Praise for

I strongly recommend *Teachables. Bite-Size Strategies That Make a Major Impact in the Classroom*. Every teacher—those new to the profession and thirty-year veterans—needs a copy of this book because there is always something we can learn to improve our performance. I wish it would have been available my first year in the classroom.

—Chris Moddelmog, MEd, executive director at Smoky Hill Education Service Center

Cheryl Abla and Lisa Maxfield have detailed meaningful and manageable instructional tactics and strategies that every teacher could apply today to support student achievement. Written by experienced educators with decades of classroom and consulting experience, this book is supported by effective research. It offers four manageable components of effective instructional approaches that can be immediately applied to enrich a school system's instructional model and a teacher's professional practice.

—Tony Davis, PhD, consultant at TDL Consulting, LLC, and former teacher and principal

Thank you, Cheryl and Lisa, for giving teachers something they really want and need! This book is user friendly and full of practical ideas and practices that require little to no prep. Great for new and veteran teachers alike. I also loved the "Above and Beyond" sections to serve as motivation and reminders for why I do what I do.

—Christy Llewellyn, instructional coach at Jellico Elementary School

Abla and Maxfield combine their experiences and wisdom to provide this must-read book for all classroom teachers. The strategies and recommendations they share apply to current or aspiring educators. The book is divided into four major components that help establish a positive learning environment for all students. This is the practical and useful book I wish I had when I started my educational career as a classroom teacher.

—Hani Youssef, superintendent of schools at Simi Valley Unified School District

The four components—YES! I appreciate how they are woven in a way that brings teaching and learning *back to the basics*. Our current reality is that many educators are at the point of overwhelm—but not because of their lack of desire to be great. Some need the tools to know *how* (the "show me" how), while others might need to find inspiration again—to discover, or rediscover—how impactful they can be for every student. This resource does both—helps to bring us back to our "why" while offering real, practical tools to know *how*. From theory to application, the extended support through technological resources, and the inclusion of personal stories—each section connects us to the *human experience* of learning. I truly can't wait to share this resource with our teachers; much more, I'm looking forward to seeing students actively engaged and learning through use of these #teachables in our classrooms!

—Joni Serisola, MEd, assistant principal at George Washington High School, Guam Department of Education

This book is a tried-and-true product of years of hard work and experience in research, learning, and teaching paired with a passion for education. I LOVE that these ladies have brought ACTUAL experiences into this book to share their wealth of knowledge with us! These practical ideas, applications, and suggestions will provide teachers with an instant advantage that will yield results. More importantly, it will enhance the classroom experience for them and their students. In a world full of resources, this one stands out as a must-have!

—Melissa Saphos, MEd, education specialist (gifted education) at Region VI ESC, Huntsville, TX, and teaching and learning adjunct professor at Sam Houston State University, Huntsville, TX

Don't you love simple solutions to complex problems? Cheryl Abla and Lisa Maxfield offer educators an expansive cornucopia of bite-sized, research-based, ready-to-implement strategies to help us address a couple common conundrums: teaching is hard, time is slippery, and this business is full of stuff that doesn't really lead to increased levels of student learning. From the moment I picked up my copy, I knew this was different. As you'll learn as you explore the hundreds of strategies, video links, resource recommendations, ideas, and tools, impactful teaching doesn't have to be difficult, time-consuming, or elaborate. It just has to make a difference, and that's what this book does.

—**Pete Hall, author of** *Always Strive to Be a Better You:* *How Ordinary People Can Live Extraordinary Lives*

Teachables: Bite-Size Strategies That Make a Major Impact in the Classroom is a valuable resource for educators who desire concrete ways to build a classroom culture centered on relationships. The book offers a menu of well-developed practical examples that can be implemented immediately and will undoubtedly transform the learning environment. Abla and Maxfield have a clear passion for education, and their engaging writing style will draw you in, inspiring and motivating you to remember everything you love about classroom teaching. I highly recommend this book to both veteran and new educators; you will be a better practitioner tomorrow having finished this book today.

—**Mrs. Chris Nelson, principal at St. Robert Bellarmine** **Catholic School, Archdiocese of Omaha**

This book truly sets itself apart with its remarkable practicality, effective organization, and ease of comprehension. What makes it even more appealing is the authors' relatability and likability, which shine through, creating an enjoyable and insightful reading experience. A standout feature of this book is its wealth of real-world examples, providing actionable insights for immediate implementation in the classroom. Whether you're a seasoned educator or embarking on your teaching journey, the strategies presented are incredibly valuable. This book is an indispensable resource for any educator who aspires to make a profound and positive impact in the classroom.

—**Grace Gutierrez, PhD, visiting assistant professor** **at the University of the Incarnate Word**

Teachables is an ingenious book that every teacher, old and new, should keep on their desktop to have quick access to strategies that really make a difference for students. Its unique format allows for reflection and community-building at every stage. Even as a veteran teacher, I was able to immediately utilize a new-to-me strategy for questioning. What an amazing resource for educators!

—Justine Rogers, gifted resource teacher at Southern Boone R-1 Schools, Ashland, MO, and adjunct instructor of English and education at Columbia College online campus

I found the book to be rooted in proven, research-based theory that is exceptionally balanced with useful strategies that are thoughtful, insightful, and can be used in the classroom from day one! In addition to all the strategies shared in the book, readers will find the personal stories, Bonus Strategies, as well as the Book Club Discussion Guide quite useful in enhancing the effectiveness of K–12 educators at any level and stage of their careers!

—Dr. Barry Harris, K–12 educator, counselor, principal, state education officer, and educational consultant in Georgia and Hawaii

An essential book for every teacher who is looking to establish positive relationships, be more organized, and increase student engagement! Cheryl and Lisa found a way to provide ready-to-use strategies for new and seasoned teachers. *Teachables* includes resources and stories that will remind you why you became a teacher, to be a positive influence in the life of children.

—Jeanette Simenson-Gurolnick, instructional coach and new teacher mentor at Aurora Public Schools, CO

I love the actionable steps for teachers that are laid out in this book. This book would be a great asset to new teachers, experienced teachers, and administrators.

—Raven Sabino, principal at Jacksboro Elementary School

This bite-size book was easy to read and full of fantastic reminders of the little things that can be changed in the classroom to make a big impact! I was super impressed.

—Sharon Norden, interrelated manager and educator with USD 259, TAP Success Coach with Wichita State University

Teachables

CHERYL ABLA AND LISA MAXFIELD

Teachables

Bite-Size Strategies
THAT MAKE A MAJOR IMPACT
in the Classroom

Published by Dave Burgess Consulting, Inc.
San Diego, CA
DaveBurgessConsulting.com

Library of Congress Control Number: 2023949137
Paperback ISBN: 978-1-956306-63-7
Ebook ISBN: 978-1-956306-64-4

Cover and interior design by Liz Schreiter
Edited and produced by Reading List Editorial
ReadingListEditorial.com

I am dedicating this book to my family and to all the students I have had the honor of teaching over the years. Thank you all for your love, patience, support, and wisdom. You have made me the person I am today and for that I love you!

—Cheryl

Thank you to my family for your love, support, and encouragement. I love you!

—Lisa/Mom/Nani XOXO

Contents

Introduction

AS EDUCATORS OURSELVES, WE KNOW YOU LOVE AND CARE ABOUT YOUR STUDENTS AND HAVE SUCCESSFUL STRATEGIES IN PLACE, BUT YOU WANT MORE. We know you want to shake things up and try something new that will make your students eager to walk through your classroom door—*every day*. We know you get up every morning to face a classroom of students who are eager, or perhaps not always so eager, to learn. We know that as you follow this calling to teach, you're up for the challenge. However, we also know it takes time to find ideas and that you have a lot going on in your life besides your classroom.

If you find yourself driven to improve as a teacher but you're pressed for time in that quest—well, you've got the right book in your hands! With *Teachables*, we've done the research and work for you. The strategies and recommendations included in this book are based on our classroom experiences as educators and observers in schools throughout the United States and on Guam, Palau, and Yap. We have spent literally hundreds of hours pulling together ideas, researching best practices, watching videos, reading books and blogs, hunting through social media, and working with countless teachers to write this book specifically for you.

Most teachers acknowledge that students' academic motivation and success are affected not just by the content you teach but also by the classroom environment you create. It makes intuitive sense that good academic outcomes rely on a foundation of a positive, thoughtfully constructed classroom culture that helps students feel ready to learn and grow, comfortable pushing themselves academically, and authentically engaged in their individual and collective learning. Our advice throughout this book centers on tips for creating the perfect classroom climate so you can build that foundation.

Focusing on your classroom environment is a good leverage point for helping students succeed. But you might have some questions: "What should I be doing in my classroom?" or "Where do I begin?" or "How do I build a positive classroom climate?" Through our observations and review of best practices, we've identified four key components for creating an enthusiastic learning environment in *all* classrooms:

1. **Relationships.** It takes trust, support, and love (yes, we said the *l*-word) to build a strong relationship with students so that they feel safe and willing to take chances while learning.

2. **Organization and Procedures.** A classroom must be organized and have clear procedures from the moment students step through the door. This consistency will create a safe environment for all students to take risks in.

3. **Curiosity and Engagement.** By trying new strategies and cultivating a classroom that engages students in the learning and gets them curious about the content, you can provide an environment where students feel excited to learn every day.

4. **High Expectations.** Having high expectations for all students is extremely powerful and helps build relationships. Students will see that with hard work and encouragement, they can do more than they may have thought possible.

In *Teachables*, we provide recommendations and action items you can use in your classroom to support these four key components. This will help you whether you teach littles, specials, gifted kids, high-need students, second-language learners, upper elementary, middle school, high school, or anything in between. We want to support you in creating a positive environment. We have also peppered personal stories through-out the book, but for the most part, we get right to the *why* and *how* to help you create your dream learning environment for all students.

Our goal is to provide concrete steps to help energize and empower you to make changes that will have a positive impact on every student in your classroom. It doesn't matter if you're a beginner or an experienced teacher—we're sure you will find new ideas. So, as you read through the strategies in this book, we hope you'll feel excited and ready to jump right in. Go ahead and start trying our recommendations; we know from experience that they will quickly make a positive difference in your classroom environment.

Lisa's Story
WHY I DIDN'T BECOME A TEACHER

AS A CHILD, WHEN I WAS ASKED WHAT I WANTED TO BE WHEN I GREW UP, THE ANSWER WAS EASY: "I WANT TO BE A TEACHER AND A PROFESSIONAL FOOTBALL PLAYER."

I believe my desire to teach started when I received a desk from my grandparents for my sixth birthday. I have a picture of me smiling, hair in long pigtails, sitting behind the desk with a red pen in my hand (clearly, my mom caught me grading papers). At some point I realized that playing in the NFL was not going to pan out for me, so my answer changed: "I'm going to be a teacher." I can still remember a friend's dad telling me, "Well you aren't going to make any money as a teacher." I responded, "I don't care about that. I want to teach kids."

Since this story is called "Why I *Didn't* Become a Teacher," you're probably wondering what happened. I'll tell you the condensed version. There was a period of my life that was not great. Don't get me wrong—the whole time wasn't bad. But for about five years, one adult who was a constant in my life definitely made it not great. He was violent and very mean, and he started calling me the *r*-word.

As you know, when anyone directs this derogatory word toward another person, it is purposely being used to be hurtful and nasty. The old saying, "Sticks and stones may break my bones, but words will never hurt me," is the biggest bunch of baloney. Horrible and offensive words hurt and cause pain that cannot be seen. As much as it angers me to admit, being called the *r*-word affected me; I lost confidence in myself and questioned my intellect. Even after that person was out of my life, the word lingered and popped up often in my mind. It had dug deep into me, though I tried to get rid of it.

Although I questioned my intelligence, I moved from Iowa and headed off to college with the goal of being a teacher. In Colorado, in order to begin taking education courses, I had to first pass a state exam. I studied for that exam every day, and though I was on a limited budget, I decided it was worth using the money I was earning at my job to hire a math tutor.

The morning of the exam, the alarm clock rang, but I turned it off, rolled over, and stayed in bed. I was sure I was going to fail the exam purely because of the mathematics section, and I was too scared to even try. So, I didn't. Afterward I felt embarrassed, but I brushed it off by saying I had decided I didn't want to be a teacher after all. This was not the truth.

After meeting Seany, my college sweetheart, getting married, and having two children (Tyler and Bodhi), I did temporarily go back to pursuing my elementary certification. By this time I had so many positives in my life that I was regaining my confidence. So, on exam day, I woke up before the alarm, jumped out of bed (I'm totally a morning person), took the exam, and passed it with flying colors. I began taking courses, writing lesson plans, and teaching preschoolers, and I absolutely loved it.

However, despite these successes, I reached the point in my teacher training where I was going to need to be gone all day, three times a week, at a school far from home. I decided I needed to pause my professional goals because I just couldn't be gone that long due to daycare and financial reasons. I needed to give up on my dream, temporarily at least, because it was best for my family. I finished college with a bachelor's degree in history but not my teaching certificate.

Now you may be wondering why I'm telling you all of this. I share this with you because I don't want you to think for even a nanosecond that I am trying to misrepresent myself as a classroom teacher who has walked in your shoes.

Yes, I taught preschool for a short time, took college-level courses, and spent hours and hours volunteering in my children's classrooms. Yes, I continually read education books and blogs, listen to podcasts, and share strategies, tips, and inspirational stories on X (formerly known as Twitter) with the educators I follow and who follow me.

But no, I never had my very own classroom. As I write this, that fact actually brings me a little sadness. However, what brings me joy (I'm all about positivity) is knowing that decisions I made created a difference in the world of education.

Since I didn't become a teacher, I have had the flexibility to take time off work and volunteer in my children's schools, helping the teachers with organizing, cleaning, grading papers, reshelving books, and cutting out whatever has needed to be cut out. You name it, I've done it. However, my favorite volunteer work at school has been reading to students and helping teach those who needed extra support with their learning. I have often been told that I missed my calling as a teacher because I clearly love working with kids and easily connect with them. In fact, kids often run up to give me a hug when I enter a classroom.

Another way I've made a difference is by working at educational organizations for over thirty years. During that time, I have helped to educate, support, and encourage teachers. I have presented at national education conferences, facilitated workshops, and written numerous blogs. In 2017 Cheryl and I designed a workshop and came up with the idea to write an activity guide for teachers to take back to their classroom. As a result of that project, we dreamed up this book to help support, encourage, and empower teachers.

So, in a nutshell, that is why I didn't become a teacher. Although I never had my own personal classroom, I have helped and supported thousands of educators to make a difference with students. My initial plan didn't come to pass, but I can honestly say I'm happy and content to be sitting where I am now.

As you continue your journey through this book, you'll have the opportunity to read more personal stories that will have you smiling, laughing, nodding, and perhaps reaching for the tissue box. The majority of the stories are from Cheryl's personal experience, but there are a few that my daughter Tyler contributed from her work as a severe needs special education teacher.

Cheryl's Story
WHY I DID BECOME A TEACHER

MY JOURNEY TO THE BEST PROFESSION OUT THERE—TEACHING—
PROBABLY BEGAN A LOT LIKE YOUR JOURNEY. At the ripe ole age of
twenty-two, I was blessed with my first class of twenty-eight ram-
bunctious third graders in Lebanon, Missouri. Fortunately, the year
prior, I was paired with the greatest classroom teacher to complete my
student teaching experience, and then I was lucky enough to take her
place when she decided to stay home with her three young children.
Her classroom and materials quickly became mine and I was on top
of the world!

When I started out, I held certain beliefs about being a classroom
teacher. I knew that relationships, and the bonds between teachers and
students, were the most important factor in helping my students to feel
that they belonged, that they were important, and that they could learn
at the highest level possible. I knew this because of the experiences I
had as a third grader.

My pedagogical inspiration came from the dearest teacher I ever
had, Mrs. Wright. Starting in first grade, I had to wear a body brace
twenty-three and a half hours a day for eight years. I had scoliosis, and
the doctors hoped the brace would hold my spine straight long enough
for me to reach an average height. Clearly this set me apart from the
other kids, and I really struggled to fit in and be a part of the class.

But things changed when I got to third grade and entered Mrs. Wright's classroom. She immediately noticed that I had a difficult time looking down at my schoolwork because of the chin guard on my brace. By the end of the first week of school, she'd had a slanted desktop made for me that was placed on top of my regular desk. For the first time in two years, I could easily see my schoolwork. What a positive difference that made for me!

Mrs. Wright also made a point to include me in all activities and not point out the differences between me and my classmates. She had a magical way of pulling me into conversations, making me feel a part of the classroom structure, and simply making me feel important and loved. The two previous years had been a struggle, but now I look back and feel extremely grateful for my parents' patience with me.

You know how you see those children clinging to their mother's knee and begging them not to leave? That was me! That ended because of the actions, beliefs, and genuine love and care Mrs. Wright provided. To this day, I am forever grateful to her. There is no doubt I am the educator and person I am now because of my school year with Mrs. Wright.

I was not always the easiest student to teach. I was not a sit-and-get type of student, and I can easily relate to students when I see them wiggling in their chairs and taking lots of water and restroom breaks. I liked hands-on learning, high engagement, and anything that included being up and active. My educators didn't always meet my needs.

When I was in fifth grade, for example, I was assigned a daily SRA (school readiness assessment). Five days a week, my class would sit in silence reading boring passages at our "specific" reading level and answering the comprehension questions. We graded our own SRAs, which meant that we all cheated. If we "improved," which we all did, we would move up to the next level.

Even as a fifth grader, I knew this wasn't effective. So, I proceeded to share with my teacher that we would all be better served if she were actively up and teaching. We couldn't genuinely improve our reading skills without help. As you may guess, this suggestion was not received very well. But at age ten, I simply couldn't understand how a teacher could sit behind their desk all day, every day, and assign busywork while expecting all of us to improve.

Given my varied experiences with education, teaching wasn't an immediate goal for me. In fact, as I headed off to college, I envisioned myself being a very strategic accountant that could balance all the spreadsheets that came across my desk. I had worked at my father's Ford/Mercury dealership in middle and high school and was quite savvy with a calculator while balancing the books. It took about a month into my first year of college to realize that wasn't for me. I wanted to make lives better by contributing in some way, and I was not going to change the world sitting behind a desk with a calculator.

I wasn't really sure how I was going to change the world, but after meeting my husband-to-be and hearing all about the classes he was taking to become a history teacher, I thought that path sounded much more impactful. I also thought about Mrs. Wright and the difference she made in my life, which made me realize that I wanted to help children learn. More than this, though, I wanted to make children happier simply because I was in their lives. So, in my second semester of college, I decided to start on the pathway to teaching. I found out quickly that this fit my goal and personality much better than accounting.

During my first years of teaching, I took what I'd liked most about school as a student and incorporated those strategies into my own classroom. At that time—1987—we didn't have the Internet, social media, webinars, or even conferences to learn better teaching strategies, so I took any chance I could to observe and learn from the engaging teachers in my school. In fact, even after years of teaching, I would still venture into my colleagues' classrooms to learn from them. Teaching can be lonely, but only if you allow it to be. As a teacher, and now as a trainer and coach, I model and encourage collaboration among teachers. We don't have to go it alone, and I have always believed that there is more to learn when it comes to improving as educators.

Those little eight-year-old third graders from my first year as a teacher in Lebanon, Missouri, are now forty-four years old. What is even more profound than the length of my time teaching is that several of my first students still keep in touch with me, which is the icing on the cake for any educator. Knowing I have made a difference in the lives of students has always been my primary focus. It's deeply rewarding that my students share their memories of how I took time to talk and play with them at recess, how we went to the care center to brighten the day for the elderly, and so many other things I don't even recall.

I have taught, coached, and worked in schools in numerous states for thirty-four years now, and my beliefs about education remain the same as on day one. As an educator, I know that we need to build strong, caring relationships with all our students. We also need to set high expectations that we genuinely believe all students can meet, and we must make school a place of excitement and happiness for both students and adults.

My hope is that as you read this book, you will select strategies to try and will reflect on your own practices. Most of all, I hope you will continue to be motivated by your students and to find joy in educating them. Teaching and learning should be fun and joyful. If it's not, change things up and create a new environment that you and your students will look forward to returning to every day!

How to Use This Book

THE MEAT OF THIS BOOK IS DIVIDED INTO THE FOUR MAJOR COMPONENTS THAT WE BELIEVE HELP TO ESTABLISH A POSITIVE LEARNING ENVIRONMENT: RELATIONSHIPS, ORGANIZATION AND PROCEDURES, CURIOSITY AND ENGAGEMENT, AND HIGH EXPECTATIONS. Within each of those four components, we offer specific strategies and recommendations. We also suggest additional materials, such as videos or articles, in the "Above and Beyond" sections.

You can easily apply our strategies within your school's instructional model or framework. Incorporating the strategies will enhance your Tier 1 instruction, which will increase student achievement.

You do not need to read this book cover to cover to begin applying the strategies. Instead, first consider which of the four components you would like to strengthen in your classroom. Next, dive into that component and select a strategy that speaks to you. Or turn to a random strategy and find the recommendation that works best for you and your students.

For each strategy we present, review the text and recommendations. Then, depending on the strategy and your comfort level, choose one of the recommendations that you believe will have the greatest positive impact on your students and implement it. As you try out recommendations, make notes for yourself about what worked (or didn't work) and what you can do differently the next time.

We believe that providing examples and hearing inspirational messages can truly enrich your understanding and learning as you enhance your classroom. Toward that end, we've provided QR codes throughout the book. Simply scan the codes with your mobile device's camera and you will be taken to a landing page on our website. There, you'll find resources, including links to articles, videos, and examples of engaging activities. Dive into a world of inspiration through our assortment of content!

Our strategies don't need to be tried in any particular order, except for the first one, "Great to See You." We recommend starting there because it's probably the easiest strategy in the book to implement and it's extremely powerful and rewarding. And really, it should be done every day, or every class period, with every student.

You've worked hard to get where you are, and you wouldn't get up every morning to educate children if you didn't want to continue to learn and develop your own skills. Our hope is that as you read this book, you highlight, make notes, self-reflect, flag or dog-ear pages, collaborate with colleagues, and dig deep to make changes in your classroom. We hope you enjoy using the strategies and recommendations we've included and that you'll share your progress with us.

Join the conversation: **#TEACHABLES**

Now, let's start where it all begins, with the first component: relationships.

> It's kind of fun to do the impossible.
> — WALT DISNEY, ANIMATOR AND ENTREPRENEUR

Chapter 1

Relationships

 RELATIONSHIPS ARE THE GLUE THAT HOLDS PEOPLE TOGETHER. Relationships are what keep employees at a particular company, the element that people remember once you are gone, and the foundation for all great songs. Have you ever thought of what your former students might say about you at your retirement party? Not just a few students— let's say they all had an opportunity to share. What would they share about their time with you? We're guessing it wouldn't be about that amazing lecture and PowerPoint on cell division; it would be about how you made them feel as a learner and as a person. Maybe they'd reflect on the respect you showed them on a daily basis or the belief you had that they could accomplish anything they put their mind to. Regardless of what their specific words might be, it would all come down to the relationship you had with them.

Depending on the grade level and content you teach, you may be spending more time each day interacting with students than they spend interacting with their parents or guardians. This provides you an opportunity to take a few moments here and there to connect with *every student, every day*. Creating a strong bond with *all* students can make a huge difference in their lives, both academically and personally.

The academic aspect of teaching is important, but having a relationship with students on a personal level—not as a friend but more as a mentor—is just as powerful. Talking with your students about their lives, cultures, hopes, dreams, or specific interests will help you to connect with them at a level that allows you to build a collaborative, engaging, and trusting environment. If you take the time to show up relationally, your students will know that you care about them as individuals.

When you think back on the teachers who had a positive impact on you and your learning, you likely recall the ones who would take the time to work with you, to discover who you were, and to learn your strengths. Those special teachers knew what was going on in your life and they cared about it, and they most likely believed that you could take on any challenge and succeed. We believe that you want to be *that* teacher for *all* students.

Above and Beyond

- Dr. Rita Pierson's eight-minute TED talk, "Every Kid Needs a Champion," has been viewed by over thirteen million people. Listen to her as she inspires us all. "I am somebody," she tells us. "I was somebody when I came. I'll be a better somebody when I leave. I am powerful, and I am strong. I deserve the education that I get here. I have things to do, people to impress, and places to go."
- Watch principal Todd Nesloney talk about the power we all have to be a cheerleader for another person—something all students deserve. Prepare to be inspired during his fifteen-minute "Kids Deserve It" TED talk.

> *Seven words that can change a kid's life:*
> *I love having you in my class.*
>
> — UNKNOWN

> *Siete palabras que pueden cambiar la vida de un niño: Me encanta tenerte en mi clase.*
>
> —— DESCONOCIDO

(We have included this quote in Spanish [from Google Translate] to model the recommendation from the "Where in the World?" strategy in section 1.7, where we advise you to use multilingual quotes in your classroom.)

Preparing to Build Relationships

Pause here for a moment and think about a student who had an impact on you. Now think about the following questions and jot down your reflections in the space below.

1. Why did that student make such an impression?

2. What made the student stand out?

3. How do you know that you had a good relationship with the student?

4. How did the relationship start and how did it blossom?

Now, look at your class roster and see if there are any students that you might need to build a stronger connection with. Take two or three minutes every day for two weeks to talk specifically to the student(s) about any topic that is outside of school. Find out who their favorite sports team or musical artist is, discover a hobby they have, or ask them about an interest that you could capitalize on to get to know them more. (See the "Quality Time" strategy in section 1.10 for more recommendations.)

> *Building relationships with students is by far the most important thing a teacher can do. Without a solid foundation and relationships built on trust and respect, no quality learning will happen.*
>
> — TIMOTHY HILTON, EDUCATOR

1.1 Great to See You: Techniques to Greet Your Students Every Day

An unfortunate reality to keep in mind is that you may be the first positive adult interaction that a student has during their day, or perhaps you're the first person to speak to them at all. An easy way to connect and build positive relationships with your students is to greet each of them every day or every class period. Welcoming students shows them how important they are to you and how happy you are to see them.

Make a point of communicating every day with every student. A simple "Hello, and how are you?" can make a huge difference in a student's life, personally and academically.

Recommendations

- Smile and greet each student by their name and use the correct pronunciation. This takes a little time at the beginning of the school year but is worth every minute.
- Say hello, good morning, or good afternoon regardless of whether the student is one of yours. This creates a welcoming and joyful school culture.
- Greet students physically. Wave, give a high five, fist-bump, show a thumbs-up, shake the student's hand, give them a pat on the shoulder, or offer them a side hug. Let the students choose how they would like to be greeted that specific day by telling you or by pointing to a picture on a poster on your classroom door.
- Have a student teach you how to pronounce hello in their native language and greet all students in that language.
- Say things like "It's great to see you," "I'm so excited you're here," or "I'm glad you're back today." This will let the student know you care about them and that they are a contributing factor in the classroom environment.
- Have a secret password that students need to say as they enter your classroom. The password can even pertain to your course content (e.g., if you're a PE teacher, the student must name an Olympic event; if you are teaching science, the student must say a science term from yesterday's lesson). This technique is a great way to acknowledge every student, and it can also be a launching point for the day's lesson or a way to clarify content that needs to be revisited.
- If you teach primary students, sit in a chair as you welcome them to the classroom so that you are at their eye level.
- Before students enter your classroom, have them "shake out the sillies" in the hallway. Give them about twenty seconds

to do this, and then they'll know that when they go into the classroom, it's time to start learning.

- Find out your students' interests and inquire about them. Examples: "How are the play rehearsals going?" or "Did you work on your car last weekend?" or "What is something new you learned at the museum?" (See the "Getting to Know You" strategy located in section 1.3.)

Above and Beyond

- The Atlanta Speech School created a powerful video from the perspective of a child. Watch their four-minute "Every Opportunity" video and think about which example best represents your school.
- Get additional tips on how to create that just-right environment for learning—where students can feel like they belong and are excited to return to the classroom each day—in Cheryl's Edutopia article "Beginning the New Year on a Positive Note."

Teachers play a crucial role in communication and connection with students, and their body language can greatly impact classroom dynamics and connectedness. A simple smile can make an enormous difference.

Please share with us on social media how you greet your students each class period or first thing in the morning. **#TEACHABLES**

Teachers who smile are better teachers.

— ASHER, SIXTH GRADER, TENNESSEE

> *Students work hardest for teachers they like and respect. When I'm asked, "How do I get the students to like and respect me?" my immediate response is, "Like and respect them first."*
>
> — Dr. Debbie Silver, educator

1.2 Caught Ya: Recognize Students for Making Good Choices

Catch your students being kind, successful, inquisitive, engaged, or helpful. When you take the time to acknowledge your students' positive actions, you build relationships and a strong risk-taking classroom environment. As the US Department of Education's Office of Safe and Healthy Students reminds us, "Students who learn in positive learning environments that are safe, supportive, and engaging are more likely to improve academically, participate more fully in the classroom, and develop skills that will help them be successful in school and in life."[1] Show you appreciate and recognize students' positive actions by communicating with the students, their peers, their parents or guardians, and other educators.

Recommendations

- Write a short, personalized note with some form of affirmation specific to the student stating what you "caught" them doing (e.g., "You really took your time and created a great website for your portfolio," "The color palette you used in your painting is creative and unique," "You held the door open for your

---

1 US Department of Education, Office of Safe and Healthy Students, *Quick Guide on Making School Climate Improvements*, National Center on Safe Supportive Learning Environments (2016). Washington, DC.

classmates," etc.). Find an opportunity to write a "caught ya" note to each student during the school year.

- Make a phone call, write a note, email, or make an appointment to video chat with the student's parents and guardians to communicate what you "caught" their child doing. This helps to continue to nurture positive relationships with your students' guardians.

- Create a "caught ya" wall and post students' names and pictures when they have shown growth, worked hard, gone above and beyond to show respect to others, made a good decision, or demonstrated a specific character trait you and your class have identified.

- Once a week, provide five minutes for students to give affirmations to one another. This will help continue to create a positive and uplifting classroom environment where students feel safe.

- As you implement "caught ya," please keep in mind that there are some students who do not want all eyes on them. They may want you to discreetly acknowledge their act. You will know which students prefer this from your conversations with them or their survey results. (See the "Getting to Know You" strategy in section 1.3.)

Note: Every single student must be recognized with a "caught ya" during the school year. Be sure to keep track because you want to recognize *all* students. Don't limit your positive affirmations to one or two actions; shoot for five or six recognitions for each student.

Affirmation Jar

To make "caught ya" a collective endeavor, introduce an affirmation jar into your classroom. You and your students can use it to acknowledge positive affirmations (e.g., acts of kindness, positive behavior, helping a classmate, and demonstrating great teamwork). All you will need is a clear jar and items such as marbles or decorative stones to place into the jar when a student is "caught." Here's how to use this strategy:

1. Explain why you are implementing the affirmation jar. Tell students it is to catch them conducting the behaviors you want to encourage or reinforce in the classroom.

2. Discuss the behaviors, actions, and goals that you want to reinforce. You can tie the expectations back to your class motto and the agreed-upon classroom expectations you developed with your students. If you haven't developed those yet, see the "This Is How We Roll" strategy in section 2.1.

3. Let students know that each time you or they see an admirable act occurring, it should be acknowledged by placing a marble into the jar and verbally announcing the act (unless the specific student does not like that type of attention). This acknowledgment can be for an individual student or for the class as a whole.

4. Set a goal prior to dropping items into the jar. Have your students provide suggestions as to what they want the reward to be when they fill the jar, and then have the class vote on the selected reward. It's important never to penalize the class by taking stones out of the jar.

5. Be deliberate about reinforcing the connection between the affirmation jar and the actions that earn a marble. The affirmation jar should be in a prominent place in your room so students see it and you can easily access it.

6. When initially introducing the jar (or jars), reward students often and consistently to build trust and create buy-in. That way, students will want to fill the jar so everyone can benefit from each other's focused work.

7. Give students positive reinforcement when they hear the sound of stones or marbles being dropped in the jar. Here are some reasons to recognize students with the affirmation jar:

- Everyone shows growth in a specific area on their benchmark assessments.
- Everyone completes their bell work on time.
- No one is tardy to class.
- The class walks in from specials and students quickly get their materials out and are ready to learn or work on their projects.
- The class receives a compliment from a specials teacher, cafeteria staff, a substitute, or another educator in the building.
- The class is collaborating and working hard on a specific project.

NOTE: This works for students of all grade levels. For middle and high school classrooms, you can use tally marks on a whiteboard (indicating each class period) or have five or six different jars (indicating which class period each jar represents).

Above and Beyond

- Warning: You may need tissues while watching a particular five-minute Spread the Love Projects video that we recommend. In it, students write positive statements about a specific classmate. When everyone has completed their affirmation, the student in question turns around and reads all the positive words their classmates have written about them. The reactions are powerful, raw, and heartwarming (hence the need for tissues).
- Consider doing this activity in your own classroom. You could devote ten minutes to it twice a week until all your students have received affirmations. Begin by showing the video to your students so they can see the effect of this exercise, and then have them try it out. As with other recognition activities, some students may feel uncomfortable having

everyone's attention focused on them. Instead of having these students stand in front of the class and read the words written about them, you could try an alternative. Have their class-mates write the words on index cards that you collect and review. Then put the notes in an envelope and hand it to the student at the end of the activity, class period, or day. (See the "Everyone? Everyone?" strategy in section 2.8 for ways to randomly choose the students.)

- Another approach would be to have your students create word clouds that you print out. This can also be a ten-minute activity twice a week. You can use FreeWordCloudGenerator.com or WordClouds.com to set up the template. Type a student's first name and then have each classmate go to the computer and type one word that describes the student. Once this is complete, print the word cloud. You can either give the document to the student that day or wait until the whole class has been described by their peers and give out all the word clouds at once.

- Design a positive "office referral" program. This needs to be coordinated with your school's administration or the main office personnel. When you have "caught" your student doing something commendable, send them to the main office with the referral. The office staff will help to celebrate the good deed by providing a certificate, tangible reward, lunch with the principal, or something students have suggested that is motivating and rewarding.

Hannah, a previous student, shared a photo of herself heading to a teaching interview while holding a jar of lemon drops. Back in her fourth-grade days, our classroom prominently featured a jar of lemon drops. Whenever students were collectively recognized for displaying good behavior or received a compliment from another teacher, they were rewarded with a lemon drop as a positive reinforcement for their exemplary behavior.

> Hi Mrs. Abla! I am on my way into a teaching interview and they told me to bring something that inspires me to be a teacher. I was thinking back and all through college when we had to think of that one teacher that always stood out, it was always you. My inspiration from the lemon drops is that I can someday be that teacher, like you were for me and hopefully there will be 22 of my students thinking about their 4th grade teacher and the impact I had on their life! So, thank you for being that teacher for me!
>
> **—HANNAH, FORMER FOURTH-GRADE STUDENT, COLORADO**

Take a picture of a note you wrote and/or your "caught ya" wall, post it on social media, and tag and follow us (we follow back). We are looking forward to hearing about all the positivity in your classroom. **#TEACHABLES**

> *The most powerful tool we have for influencing behavior is the relationship we build with kids.*
>
> CASEY O'ROARTY, POSITIVE DISCIPLINE TRAINER AND PARENT COACH

1.3 Getting to Know You: Survey Students to Build Connections

To build relationships with students, it is important to know about their lives. What are their passions? What gets them curious? What are some of their struggles? Creating a community and safe space can help you personalize learning and solidify relationships.

The best way to build relationships with students is simply to ask them questions about themselves. The small investment of time this takes will pay off the entire semester or school year. Regardless of how much content you need to cover, always take the time to ask students about themselves.

Recommendations

- Create a simple interest survey, either physically with pen and paper or digitally with HubSpot, KwikSurveys, SurveyPlanet, Google Forms, SurveyMonkey, or Jotform. Students can write or draw their responses to this survey (depending on the format and the student's age). Remind students that you will not share their personal responses and that the survey is for your eyes only. However, as long as questions are not too personal, you can use some of the responses to craft lessons and projects based on students' interests and passions. This survey can take ten to fifteen minutes to complete and will provide you with a wealth of information to help you connect with every one of your students.
  - Example questions:
    - What is your favorite hobby?
    - Who do you follow on TikTok?
    - Who is your favorite sports team?
    - What is your favorite subject in school?

- What is the title of your favorite book?
- What are you most passionate about?
- What is your biggest fear?
- What do you like/dislike about school?
- What is something you think I should know to help you learn the best you can in our classroom?
- How do you learn best?
- How do you like to be recognized?
- What helps you stay focused?

- Take the survey yourself and share your responses with your students. You can share answers over a couple of weeks or months so that students will be wondering what they'll learn next about you. When you share one of your own responses, you can ask your students if they would like to share their response to that specific question.

- Use a digital platform like Seesaw to pose a couple of "getting to know you" video questions. Have your students respond in video form and allow them to comment on one another's answers, if appropriate.

- Create a question cube (e.g., a wooden block, foam cube, or cube made from cardstock) with questions on each side that students answer after they roll it. Use images to accommodate the needs of all your students (e.g., second-language learners, students in special education, primary age students). This is an interactive way to engage students at all grade levels in getting to know one another.

- Randomly play Two Truths and a Lie during the school year. First, ask a student to provide two truths and a lie. After the student has made three statements, the class needs to determine which statement is the lie. Keep track of which students have provided statements throughout the year and be sure to also join in the fun yourself. This is a great way for students to interact with one another, and it's a wonderful two-minute brain break. Of course, students can always choose not to participate. (This is also in the "My Story" strategy found in section 1.5.)

Building Collaboratively

Have your students create a structure while you observe their strengths and collaboration skills. This activity is great for all grade levels.

1. Have your students gather in random teams of three or four, or see the strategy "Everyone? Everyone?" in section 2.8 for ways to randomly group students.
2. Provide students with around twenty spaghetti noodles and a handful of small marshmallows.
3. Tell the class they will have ten minutes to design and create the tallest structure in the classroom.
4. Take notes on who the leaders are, who sits back, who takes directions well, and who struggles to jump into the activity. This information will provide you with great insight into who has strong communication and/or collaboration skills. It will also help you design future grouping protocols.

Building Emotional Intelligence

Emotional intelligence (EQ) is about understanding and controlling emotions in oneself and others. Teaching EQ provides students with vital social and emotional skills like empathy, self-awareness, and relationship building. These skills are crucial for personal and academic success. Here are some strategies that you can incorporate to develop and enhance your students' EQ:

- Promote a supportive and inclusive classroom atmosphere where students feel safe to express themselves and share their thoughts and emotions. Encourage mutual respect, active listening, and empathy among students.

- Make sure you serve as a role model for your students. Demonstrate emotional intelligence by effectively managing your own emotions, displaying empathy, and resolving conflicts in a constructive manner. Students learn by observing your behavior and actions.

- Encourage students to consider the feelings and perspectives of others. Engage them in activities that promote understanding and empathy, such as discussing diverse cultures and experiences.

- Guide students in recognizing and managing their emotions effectively. Teach them strategies like deep breathing exercises, mindfulness techniques, or taking breaks when they feel overwhelmed. Help them understand that it's normal to experience a range of emotions and provide tools to cope with difficult ones.

- Engage students in problem-solving activities that require them to consider different viewpoints, think critically, and find solutions that benefit all parties involved. This helps them develop empathy, perspective, and decision-making skills.

- Be attuned to your students' emotional well-being and offer support when needed. Promote open lines of communication, encourage students to reach out if they need help, and connect them with appropriate resources such as school counselors.

Above and Beyond

- Hamish Brewer is known as the relentless, tattooed, skateboarding principal. Watch his passionate sixteen-minute TEDxChristchurch video, "How Radical Love Transformed a School," and listen to him talk about love, respect, and legacy.

- We have created a survey for you to share with your students or use as a starting point to create your own. Go to our website to download *Example Student Survey*.

Do you think students understand the purpose of school? It's a great question to ask them, and you can group the responses into different categories. If you want to take it one step further, place the students with the most common answers in a group and have them discuss their thoughts. Then, have a whole-class discussion based on that one simple question. Ask clarifying questions, pose questions based on student responses, and if the whole group can come to a consensus, make that a class motto. If they can't come to a consensus, use a thinking prompt to engage in a deeper debate (e.g., "What evidence do you have to back up your claim?").

Here is a response from a student:

> The purpose of school is not just to learn but become a better human being. Sure, you also need to know your math and history facts. But the point of school is to gain skills like compassion, self-awareness, organization, and kindness. That is a teacher's ultimate goal.

> —CYNTHIA, SEVENTH GRADER, CALIFORNIA

Please share with us on social media what you did to get to know your students this school year. Let us know how it worked! #TEACHABLES

> *Life is about the opportunity that you get to impact the world around you, to make a difference, to leave a legacy.*
>
> — HAMISH BREWER, EDUCATOR

1.4 Communicate, Communicate, Communicate: Foster Relationships with Parents and Guardians

It's important to start building positive relationships with students as soon as possible, and communicating with their parents or guardians is a great way to connect and provide transparency. Reaching out to parents or guardians before the school year starts, and again throughout the year, helps to create a partnership with the goal of helping their child learn. It also shows the student and their parents or guardians that you are excited about teaching and have the motivation to help the student succeed.

Recommendations

- Make a positive call home to students' parents or guardians within the first couple of weeks of school (for elementary grades) or within the first month (for secondary students). Yes, that's a lot of phone calls for secondary teachers, but this simple gesture will pay off for the rest of the semester or school year.
- If there is a language barrier between you and a student's parents or guardians, use an online translation tool to communicate in the student's native language. Even if your wording isn't perfect, your effort will make a difference. Google Translate, Microsoft Translator, and the Bing translator are examples of options that you can use.

- Use the convenient communications applications your school has in place (e.g., Remind, ClassDojo, Infinite Campus) to connect with specific families or everyone. The platforms are also a safe way to regulate family and student messages.
- Hold an evening meeting (thirty to forty-five minutes) with your students' parents and guardians the first month of school and call it something like "Tricks for Success" or "Set for Success." Provide specific resources, guidance, and tools that attendees can use at home to support their child during the semester or school year. This meeting can be done in person, via a recording, or through a live webinar. Remember, not all parents and guardians may be able to attend, but that doesn't mean they don't still want the information.

Note: Continue to communicate with parents and guardians even if you don't receive responses to your calls, notes, newsletters, or emails. Some parents and guardians may choose to not get involved, while others can't because of work, other children, responsibilities, health, etc. Keep the communication flowing.

Face-to-Face Time

Create a short (three to five minutes) recording of yourself so parents and guardians can see and hear your enthusiasm for teaching and learning. Share the link with them prior to the start of school or in the first couple of days. When creating your video, it's essential to include relevant information that helps them understand and support their child's educational journey. Here are some elements for you to consider including in the video:

- Share your experience as an educator and why you love being a teacher.
- Provide an overview of the curriculum and what their child will be learning.

- Share your style of teaching and how you like to keep students engaged in their learning experience.
- Tell them the expectations you have for your students and explain your grading system and how you provide feedback. Provide information regarding your homework and assignment policies.
- Describe how you run your classroom and how you model and expect a safe learning environment for all.
- Request that they complete a parent survey and tell them why it is important for you to receive a response.
- Let them know how to contact you and the hours you are available.

Read All about It

Design a short weekly or monthly newsletter to keep communication lines open with families. If you teach upper elementary or high school, you can have your students contribute to the newsletter. Here are some suggestions on what you can include:

- Present an overview of what your class has learned since the previous newsletter.
- Highlight the upcoming focus of instruction and let them know what their child will be learning.
- Provide information about upcoming deadlines or events.
- Share resources that would be helpful to them to support their child's learning.
- Celebrate! Acknowledge individual students throughout the school year and share why they are being recognized. Make a list and be sure that every student gets recognized for something they accomplished or an act of kindness.
- Encourage parents and guardians to communicate with you if they have any questions or concerns. Provide your contact

information and the hours you are available for a phone call, videoconference, or in-person meeting.

- Use bullet points and visuals to make the newsletter appealing. It should be concise and take only a few minutes to read.

Staying in Touch

Some teachers like to move beyond the traditional newsletter. Here are three effective alternatives to consider for reaching parents and guardians:

- Use a videoconferencing platform (e.g., Zoom, Google Meet, Skype) to host a regular meeting with parents and guardians to provide updates and information about what is happening in their child's classroom. You can make these meetings more engaging by having a guest speaker. Many parents are looking for support and guidance. Having a child development expert talk about specific subjects (e.g., help with reading, communicating with your teenager) would be beneficial.

- Podcasts are super popular, so why not try your hand at communicating through one? Find a topic that would be relevant and interesting to your audience of parents and guardians. You could speak on the topic or, better yet, conduct interviews with guests, such as a current or former student, a colleague, or an expert.

- Create a social media classroom page to disseminate important information. The content would be similar to a newsletter, but you would be able to update it more regularly and include additional material. Parents and guardians would be able to ask questions and interact with you through this page, which could strengthen communication. Before setting this up, you would need to make sure that you have parent or guardian consent to post images with their child's face. Additionally, there would need to be clear guidelines regarding the privacy and security of the page.

Ask Away

Create a survey to send to parents and guardians to find out more about their child and to confirm the best way to communicate. This information will help you start building a strong relationship with all parties involved. Here are some example questions you can ask:

- How does your child feel about school?
- How can I best help your child?
- What extracurricular activities does your child do?
- Which communication channels do you prefer for receiving general updates and announcements from me?
- How often would you like to receive updates regarding your child's academic progress and classroom activities?

There are many online tools available that can help you create surveys for students' families. Here are a couple of options:

- Google Forms is free (bonus!) and allows you to create customized surveys. It offers a variety of question types, customizable themes, and the ability to analyze responses within Google Sheets.
- SurveyMonkey provides a lot of features and options to help you create surveys. There is a free version, but if you want advanced options, you'll have to pay for a subscription.

Above and Beyond

- FutureMe.org allows you to set a specific date for an email to be sent to you in the future. Why not use that tool to write a letter to yourself at the beginning of the school year? What are your hopes and dreams? What goals do you have for yourself and your classroom? You can also write this letter on a piece of paper, put it in an envelope, and leave it in your desk drawer. Then, set a reminder on your phone for the day you want to read it. Plan to read the letter in the spring, as you might need a reminder of your passion for teaching toward the end of the school year. (Note: FutureMe.org is also in the "My Story" strategy found in section 1.5.)

> We can't overstress the importance of communicating with your students' families. Primary, elementary, middle school, high school . . . The families are sending you their most cherished treasure. Families need to be communicated with even when you aren't certain they are hearing, reading, or seeing your message. It matters!
>
> Receiving notes from current or former students is meaningful, similar to the deep sense of pride derived from notes received from parents.
>
>> Cheryl Abla we have you to thank first. You have been like no other educator our kids have had. You always inspired, played music (I mean, Adrianna came home singing Come Sail Away!), taught with passion and encouraged our kids. They were lucky to have you. Thank you for the seeds you've planted. You've truly made a difference. ♥ Adriana was with you 4th through 6th grade. If only all kids had a Mrs. Abla!
>>
>> **—RENEE, FORMER PARENT, COLORADO**

After you've made positive phone calls home, created a podcast, or written a newsletter, please tell us on social media how it made you feel and share the best response you received from a family member. Tag us, please. **#TEACHABLES**

> *It is teachers who have created positive teacher student relationships that are more likely to have the above average effects on student achievement.*
>
> — JOHN HATTIE, EDUCATOR AND RESEARCHER

1.5 My Story: Building Positive Relationships by Sharing Our Stories

You're curious about your students' lives—and they're curious about yours. The "My Story" strategy is a great way to strengthen relationships with and among your students, and it helps you build a safe and cohesive learning environment.

According to principal Helena Marsh, students have stated that having personal interactions with teachers who "show their own personal preference and interests and show that they have a life outside of teaching"[2] helps with a positive teacher-student relationship. In other words, students need to know that you are human and not perfect. Sharing your story is a great way to help them see that not everything was easy for you either.

Don't just tell students about your successes; share times in which you worked hard and still failed at something. This helps set the tone for a year of taking risks to learn new things. You will first present your story, and then your students will create theirs. You can provide the template we have shared or create your own guidelines to best meet your students' needs.

---

2   Helena Marsh, "Relationships for Learning: Using Pupil Voice to Define Teacher-Pupil Relationships That Enhance Pupil Engagement," *Management in Education* 26, no. 3 (July 2012): 162.

The "My Story" Model

- Model "My Story" for your students by creating *your* story first.
  - Use a poster board or a technological tool to tell your story.
  - Add pictures and don't forget to include the silly and embarrassing ones. Your students will love to laugh at (we mean *with*) you.
  - Include a picture of yourself at their age.
  - Share facts such as where you were born or grew up, how many siblings you have, and the occupations of your parents or guardians.
  - Reveal your biggest accomplishment and how you reached it, and also share a failure or regret you have.
  - Share why you became a teacher and why you love to teach.
- Next, create a "My Story" template with specific information the students will share and consider implementing technology (e.g., PowerPoint, Powtoon, Scribe). To help you get started, we have created a "My Story" PowerPoint template that you can access on our website.
- Have students create presentations about themselves. This is a great way for them to find connections with classmates who have similar experiences or interests.
- Another option is to have students practice their listening and presentation skills by pairing up to create a "My Story" about their partner. They will have ten minutes to interview their classmate, listen to responses, and take notes. Students will then use technology to create a two-minute presentation about the person they interviewed using the template you provided.

Recommendations

- Have the occasional Hidden Talent Tuesday, where students can sign up to share a talent they have. You should share one too. Take pictures of them rolling their tongues, bending their thumbs backward, or displaying whatever their talent might be. Post the pictures in the classroom or hallway—with their permission, of course.

- Create a wall with pictures of your students (again with their permission). This is an excellent way to show students that they belong in your classroom, that you see them as contributing individuals, that you value their ideas, and that your classroom is inclusive of everyone who enters.

- Help your students connect with one another by talking to each other. This can provide a nice brain break. You could have students ask questions such as "Where is one place you want to visit?" or "What is your favorite song?" Play music and have the students walk around the room. When the music stops, everyone asks the person closest to them their question. As the school year progresses, students will learn more and more about one another, which will build community, a safe environment, and a structure for processing new learning.

- Randomly play Two Truths and a Lie during the school year. First, ask a student to provide two truths and a lie. After the student has made three statements, the class needs to determine which statement is the lie. Keep track of which students have provided statements throughout the year and be sure to also join in the fun yourself. Of course, students can always choose not to participate. (This is also in the "Getting to Know You" strategy located in section 1.3.)

Future Writing

Have your students use FutureMe.org to write a letter that will be emailed to their future self. The letter can be delivered any time they choose (e.g., six months, one year, ten years). Alternatively, have them write a letter and/or goals at the beginning of the school year that you will distribute during the last day of class. Here are some prompts to get your students writing:

- What are your current dreams and aspirations? Write about how you envision yourself achieving them in the future.
- Describe your favorite hobbies and interests.
- Write about your closest friends and the memories you've shared. Reflect on the importance of friendships and how they might have changed over time.
- What challenges or obstacles are you currently facing? Write about how you hope to overcome them and what advice you would give your future self.
- Reflect on your current strengths and weaknesses. How do you imagine they will shape your future self?
- Write about a significant life event or accomplishment that you hope to achieve in the future. Describe the steps you plan to take to make it a reality.
- Imagine your ideal future career. Write about the path you're currently on and how it aligns with your aspirations.
- Reflect on your personal growth and self-improvement journey. What lessons have you learned so far, and what do you hope to achieve in the future?
- Write about the relationships you have with your family members. How do you envision them evolving as time goes on?
- Imagine yourself ten years from now. What do you hope your life looks like? Describe your ideal future lifestyle, including your home, travel experiences, and personal achievements.

Feel free to choose one or combine multiple prompts to create a comprehensive letter. (This is also in the "Communicate, Communicate, Communicate" strategy found in section 1.4.)

Above and Beyond

- Read the book "The Best Part of Me" by Wendy Ewald to your class. This book beautifully explains how we are all different yet beautiful in our own way. Encourage students of all ages to write a descriptive paragraph about their favorite body part. Snap a black-and-white photo of each student's favorite body part to showcase with their paragraph. This practice is an empowering journey of self-acceptance. By focusing on the parts they love, students cultivate self-esteem, embrace their individuality, and foster a positive body image. This creative activity promotes self-expression, inclusivity, and personal growth, allowing students to develop a deeper understanding of themselves and celebrate their unique beauty.

- Brené Brown's TED talk "The Power of Vulnerability" has gained widespread popularity and recognition for good reason. She discusses topics such as personal growth, emotional resilience, and overcoming fear and shame. Both teachers and high school students can benefit from her valuable insights and practical advice by watching this twenty-minute talk.

> There is nothing more important than knowing how to build strong, positive relationships with the students you connect with daily. Students will always go above and beyond when they know you genuinely care about them.

We would love to hear what you do to build strong relationships with your students. Which relationship-building strategies did you try? Please let us know on social media how it went and what the results were. **#TEACHABLES**

> *Vulnerability is not winning or losing;*
> *it's having the courage to show up and*
> *be seen when we have no control over*
> *the outcome.*
>
> — BRENÉ BROWN, PROFESSOR AND AUTHOR

1.6 Thankful Thursday: Being Grateful Creates a Positive Mindset

You know that feeling when you receive a handwritten note from a friend, family member, or student? It brings a smile to your face, and you put it on your desk, keep it in your "special folder," or place it where you can read it often.

Thankful Thursday is an excellent way to teach your students the importance of gratitude by letting others know they are appreciated. An act of kindness leaves the contributor and the recipient feeling all warm and fuzzy inside.

Recommendations

- Once a month, give students a few minutes to write a thank-you note. The note can be written to anyone they choose: a classmate, a family member, another teacher, a former teacher, you (because you are wonderful), cafeteria staff, or even themselves. They should be sure to mail or deliver the note to the person.

- Have your students record a brief (one to two minutes) thank-you message on Zoom, TikTok, or Instagram to share with the person to whom they are grateful. A written note is wonderful, but it's beautiful to see someone's facial expression as words of gratitude are spoken.
- On occasional Thursdays, bring your students together in a circle and have each one state what they are thankful for at that moment. This should take no more than five minutes, and it sets a positive tone for the class period or day.
- Create a "gift of kindness" bulletin board and post various acts of kindness onto the board. Students can contribute their creative ideas to the board as well. Each week, introduce a new random act of kindness for students to carry out. Encourage reflection through writing or sharing stories, and assess whether acts of kindness are creating a positive change to their day. Here are some examples of random acts of kindness that your students can try:
  - Write positive messages and post them around the classroom or school.
  - Say thank you to school staff (e.g., bus drivers, custodial, cafeteria, and front office).
  - Invite a classmate you don't typically eat with to join you at lunch.
  - Write a note to a family member telling them how they had a positive impact on you.
  - Give a compliment to someone you don't normally talk to.
  - Call a relative on the phone and ask them questions about their life.
- Create a "shout out" board and provide colorful paper for students to anonymously write positive affirmations for one another. This promotes a culture of encouragement and motivation. Seeing positive affirmations from their peers can uplift

students' spirits, boost their self-confidence, and inspire them to excel in their endeavors. It acts as a constant reminder that their efforts are recognized and valued by others, which can have a profound impact on their academic and personal growth. (See the "Caught Ya" strategy in section 1.2 for additional recommendations.)

Above and Beyond

- Watch the eight-minute "Random Acts of Kindness in School: The Breakfast Club" video. See what a difference a group of eighth-grade students made in their school. Oh, and you may need tissues for this one. If appropriate, share with your students.
- The Random Acts of Kindness Foundation website provides free lesson plans, coloring pages, quotes, posters, videos, and more to use in your classroom. They have loads of ideas on how to spread kindness any day of the year (e.g., send an uplifting text, give an unexpected gift, pick up litter). And be sure to mark these two days on your calendar now:
  - February 17: Random Acts of Kindness Day
  - November 13: World Kindness Day

Gratitude accompanies generosity and empathy, so when students possess a sense of gratitude for the things they have in life, it tends to inspire them to engage in acts of kindness toward others. This creates a cycle of positivity which also builds a strong sense of community and compassion.

Share on social media some of your successful Thankful Thursday activities. If you have other ideas, please share those as well. Be sure to tag us. **#TEACHABLES**

> *By trying to make ourselves happier and more successful, we actually have the ability to improve the lives of 1,000 people around us.*
>
> — SHAWN ACHOR, AUTHOR

1.7 Where in the World?: Celebrating Diversity as an Opportunity for Learning

The "Where in the World?" strategy provides a fabulous opportunity for students to learn about their classmates in broader contexts.

Zaretta Hammond, an expert on culturally responsive teaching, states that surface culture "is made up of observable and concrete elements of culture such as food, dress, music, and holidays. This level of culture has a low emotional charge so that changes don't create great anxiety in a person or group."[3] By extension, implementing surface-level activities will allow students to see and hear similarities and differences between themselves and their classmates. Take the time to discuss and celebrate diversity with your students.

Recommendations

- Display a map of the world and have students place a pin where their ancestors originated. Use the information from the map to explore students' traditions and customs.
- Read books and articles about other cultures and regions.
- Provide a library with diverse books. (See the "Have You Read This? You Have to Read This!" strategy found in section 3.4.)
- Celebrate regions and countries with flags, food, passport projects, clothing, music, games, art, and dance.

---

3   Zaretta L. Hammond, *Culturally Responsive Teaching and the Brain: Promoting Authentic Engagement and Rigor among Culturally and Linguistically Diverse Students* (Thousand Oaks, CA: Corwin, 2014), 22.

- Create and display posters of successful individuals from all over the world.
- Display posters of multilingual quotes.
- Discuss how some common words vary depending on where you are in the world. For example, in the US a soft drink is referred to as a pop, soda, cola, or Coke. What do people outside of the US call a soft drink? Have your students find other examples.
- Have students work in groups to research a country and share findings that are related to course material (e.g., in health class they can research which state or country has the most bike paths).
- Play music in different languages and from different regions.
- Allow students to bring in an item or picture that represents their heritage. Ask them to share stories about the item and tell the class why it reminds them of their culture.

Passport Project

A passport project can be a fun educational activity. It allows students to explore different countries, cultures, and geographies while being creative and practicing research and presentation skills. Here are suggestions on how to create a passport project:

1. **Set the objective.** Clearly define the goals of the passport project. Are you focusing on geography, culture, history, or a combination? Determine what you want students to learn and achieve through this project.
2. **Choose a region or country.** Provide a region or a list of countries for students to research and include in their passports.
3. **Research.** Guide students in researching each country's geography, culture, history, landmarks, language, and traditions. Encourage them to find interesting facts and details that will make their passports informative and engaging.

4. **Create passport booklets.** Provide each student with a template or instructions on creating a passport booklet. If you're not using a premade template, the booklet can be made using folded sheets of paper. Include pages for personal information, visa stamps, and country-specific information.

5. **Gather information.** Incorporate specific requirements for each country's page, such as a flag, famous landmarks, cultural practices, and interesting facts. Students can write descriptions, draw or print images, and include maps.

6. **Add visual elements.** Encourage creativity by having students add drawings, individual images, or collages to represent each country. They can include pictures of landmarks, traditional clothing, flags, food, and more.

7. **Create passport stamps.** To make the project more interactive, have students create "passport stamps" for each country. These can be stamps or stickers that signify a visit to that country. This adds an element of fun and a sense of accomplishment.

8. **Present.** Have students present their completed passport projects to the class. They can share interesting facts, cultural insights, and their personal experience "traveling" to each country.

9. **Host a cultural showcase.** Consider hosting a cultural showcase event where students display their passports and provide additional information about the regions or countries they researched. This could include traditional food samples, music, or displays of artifacts.

10. **Assess.** Develop a rubric to assess the quality of each student's passport project. Consider factors such as accuracy of information, creativity, presentation skills, and effort put into the project.

11. **Assign extension activities.** To deepen learning, you can assign follow-up activities like writing reflective essays,

creating multimedia presentations, or comparing different countries.

12. **Display and celebrate.** Create a bulletin board or display area where students can showcase their completed passport projects. Celebrate their hard work and the diversity of cultures represented.

Remember, the passport project should be an engaging and enjoyable learning experience. Adapt the suggestions based on the grade level, resources available, and specific learning objectives you want to achieve.

Celebrating diversity in the classroom will promote an inclusive and equitable learning environment. By modeling acceptance of others, you can help students appreciate different cultures, perspectives, and backgrounds, which will help promote empathy, respect, and understanding of one another.

On social media, share with us which recommendation(s) you tried from the "Where in the World?" strategy. If you have pictures to share, we would love to see them. Oh, and please follow (we follow back, of course) and tag us. **#TEACHABLES**

> *Culturally responsive teaching is about helping culturally and linguistically diverse students who have been marginalized in schools build their skill and capacity to do rigorous work. The focus isn't on motivation but on improving their brainpower and information processing skills.*
>
> — ZARETTA HAMMOND, EDUCATOR AND AUTHOR

1.8 Walk in My Shoes: Build Empathy to Build Community

We've all heard the saying "You should walk in my shoes." There's a good reason to at least visualize the circumstances of another person: this practice helps build empathy. As an adult, you know that empathy is the capacity to understand and share the feelings of another person. But do your students understand and show empathy toward others? Take advantage of opportunities to model, discuss, and practice empathy to help students become more empathetic.

You can do this through storytelling in your classroom. Use real situations, like a time when you judged someone for their unpleasant attitude only to find out later that they had a family member in the hospital or were going through another traumatic event. It doesn't dismiss that person's unpleasantness, but it does show that it might not have been intentional. Below are some great recommendations to help you teach your students about empathy.

Recommendations

- Find a short (one to two minutes) audio or video clip in a different language of your choosing. Prior to sharing it with your students, tell them that after listening to or viewing the clip, they will write a summary of what they heard. When you start the clip, watch their expressions and reactions as they realize they are not hearing English. When the clip ends, start a discussion about how they felt when they didn't understand the language. Help them connect this with the idea of walking in the shoes of someone who is surrounded by English speakers but who does not speak English. This can be a powerful activity to help build empathy and a culture of belonging for all students.

- Depending on the age of your students, have them draw or write about the topic of "I wish my teacher knew . . ." Reading students' letters, or viewing their drawings, allows you to gain insights into the diverse backgrounds and experiences of your students. This promotes a sense of empathy and helps you recognize the unique challenges and strengths that each student brings to the classroom. It also encourages a more inclusive and supportive environment where students feel valued and respected for who they are.

- Show pictures of people to your students and ask them how they think that person may have felt as a result of the circumstances shown in the photos. You can use famous photos, e.g., Christopher Reeve, Tank Man, Mary Decker at the 1984 Olympics, Louis Armstrong playing the trumpet, *Afghan Girl*, *Cotton Mill Girl*, etc. This is another way to help build empathy and perspective with your students. For example, show the *Migrant Mother* picture taken by Dorothea Lange. This photo depicts Florence Owens Thompson, a destitute mother of seven children, looking tired and worried as she holds her young children close to her. This photograph has become a symbol of the hardships faced by many during the Great Depression and has come to represent the struggles of poverty and the human capacity for resilience. The photo captures the emotions of a mother trying to provide for her family in desperate circumstances, eliciting compassion from viewers. It serves as a powerful reminder of the importance of empathy in recognizing and responding to the struggles faced by individuals and communities in crisis. By examining photographs, students can delve into the themes of empathy, social inequality, and the power of visual storytelling. They can discuss the challenges faced by marginalized communities and the importance of understanding and addressing the needs of those experiencing poverty.

- Music lyrics can teach students about empathy and the perception of others. They employ storytelling and emotional expression, and they can address social issues, promote personal reflection, and bolster an appreciation of diversity. Music can also work magic on our heartstrings, helping students connect with their own emotions. Play a song to your students and ask what the lyrics mean to them and why they think the songwriter wrote them. (See the "Play the Music" strategy in section 3.10 on how to create a "Lyric Lesson.")
- Explore music from diverse backgrounds to help students cultivate an appreciation for different cultures. Emotional depth in music helps students recognize and empathize with diverse feelings, broadening their perception of others' experiences even if the song is in another language.

Playing at Empathy

Elementary students enjoy creating skits to show their understanding of content, so have your students create one about what they should do when they see someone who needs their support and empathy (e.g., an elderly person, a person with a disability, a new classmate). Here are the steps for this activity:

1. Start by introducing the activity to your students (allocate fifteen minutes for this). Explain that they will be creating a short skit (three to five minutes) to demonstrate how they can show support and empathy when they encounter someone in need. Emphasize that skits are a fun and creative way to showcase their understanding of the content.
2. Engage the students in a brainstorming session (thirty minutes). Encourage them to think about various situations where they might come across someone in need of support and empathy. Prompt them to consider what these encounters

might look, feel, and sound like. Encourage open dialogue and active participation to promote creativity and empathy.

3. Divide the students into small groups, assigning each group a specific scenario from the brainstorming session. In their groups, have the students work together to develop a script for their skit (sixty minutes). Encourage them to consider the actions, dialogue, and emotions involved in showing support and empathy. Remind them to keep their skits between three and five minutes long.

4. Allocate time for the groups to rehearse their skits (fifteen minutes). Allow them to practice their lines, gestures, and movements. Encourage the students to provide constructive feedback to one another, focusing on how the skits effectively demonstrate support and empathy. Help them refine their performances by offering suggestions and guidance.

5. Give each group an opportunity to perform their skits in front of the class or a larger audience, such as other students, teachers, or parents. After each performance, facilitate a reflection session where students can share their thoughts and feelings about the skits. Encourage them to discuss the different ways support and empathy were portrayed and how it made them feel. Use this opportunity to reinforce the importance of empathy and discuss the impact it can have on others. (Allocate approximately sixty minutes for all group performances plus reflection time.)

Remember to adapt these steps to suit the age and abilities of your students. Encourage creativity, collaboration, and reflection throughout the process to create a meaningful and impactful experience.

Above and Beyond

- Watch Jonathan Juravich's ten-minute TED talk, "How Do You Teach Empathy?" He speaks about his experiences with his loving grandmother as well as teaching empathy and how to make it actionable.

- View the twelve-minute TED talk "Help for Kids the Education System Ignores" and listen to the strategies presented by Dr. Victor Rios. By exploring innovative teaching approaches, he equips viewers with practical strategies to cultivate empathy in their own lives and empower the next generation. Understanding the power of empathy and learning actionable ways to implement it will not only enhance your personal growth but also contribute to creating a more compassionate and connected world.
- We have started a reading list that includes elementary-level books on empathy. Additionally, Common Sense Media and Goodreads have comprehensive lists of books on empathy.
- We've also compiled a list of videos that show the power of empathy. Review each video to determine if it's appropriate to show to your students.
  - Elementary-level empathy videos:
    - In a one-minute video called "Children in Karate Class Cheer Kid on While Kicking Board," watch as children encourage their classmate to break a board in karate class. This video fosters a supportive classroom environment where students learn to uplift and motivate one another. By witnessing the children's encouragement, students can understand the power of positive peer influence and the value of teamwork. Additionally, the video showcases the determination and resilience required to achieve personal goals, inspiring students to persevere in their own endeavors.
    - A five-minute video called "All About Empathy (for kids!)" teaches students what empathy is, why it's important, and how to start practicing it. By

watching the video, students can gain a clear understanding of empathy's significance in nurturing positive relationships. They can also learn how to begin implementing empathy as a practice in their daily lives. The video's brevity and practical tips make it an effective tool for introducing empathy and encouraging students to cultivate a more compassionate mindset.

- ○ Secondary-level empathy videos:
  - A twelve-minute video called "Immersion" offers a unique perspective, allowing students to witness firsthand the challenges and experiences faced by a non-English-speaking student. This video will enhance empathy and understanding toward peers who are learning a new language. By showing this video, you can promote inclusivity, encourage cultural sensitivity, and foster a supportive classroom environment.
  - Watch a powerful four-minute video, "Under the Surface," which gives examples of unseen challenges that students and school personnel may be experiencing. The video helps raise awareness about hidden struggles, fostering empathy and understanding. It encourages dialogue, promotes a supportive community, and provides resources for addressing mental health concerns effectively.
  - A two-minute video called "Burger King Anti-bullying PSA" will raise awareness about the issue of bullying among teenagers and promote empathy and compassion among students. By showcasing the impact of bullying on both individuals and the community, the video can initiate

meaningful discussions and encourage students to take a stand against bullying.

- A two-minute video titled "Offer Empathy" illustrates the transformative power of empathy by depicting positive shifts in the lives of individuals who receive empathetic support. Through simple acts of understanding and compassion, the video demonstrates the profound impact empathy can have on people's circumstances and emotional well-being.

  ○ Empathy videos for any level:
    - Check out a one-minute video called "Pub Fosterhjem: A child has nothing to eat at school." It raises awareness about food insecurity, prompting discussions on empathy, compassion, and the importance of helping others in need. It serves as a powerful reminder of the privileges many students may take for granted, fostering gratitude and working as a call to action to make a positive difference in one's community.
    - View "Understanding Special Needs Children," a five-minute video created by the Polka Dot Project. It helps students learn empathy by providing a unique and engaging perspective that promotes understanding, compassion, and awareness of the challenges faced by special needs children. It encourages students to put themselves in others' shoes and cultivate empathy.

In a charter school with a predominantly Latino/a population, a young teacher's love for books created a ripple effect of empowerment and support. What began as a simple act of lending a book evolved into an unofficial book club that then transformed into an undocumented support group, providing vital information and solace to students living in fear of deportation. Years later, a grateful mother reached out, expressing her deep appreciation for the teacher's unwavering support and the profound impact she had on her son's life.

The charter school I taught at for two years had a very high Latino/a population. One of my students noticed that I always had a book on me and asked if I liked it. I was reading "In The Country We Love" by Diane Guerrero. I told the student a bit about the book and she was very interested so I bought the young adult version of the book and let her borrow it. She then told another student and let her borrow it.

Soon I had a group of about eight girls asking for more books, specifically ones that dealt with deportation, the undocumented experience, and Latina voices. We formed an unofficial book club and would meet during lunch. Other students found out and asked to join. All of these students feared deportation either for themselves or someone that they loved. Because of this I found contacts in the community so I could give them information to keep them safe. Our unofficial book club ended up being an unofficial undocumented support group. Being able to be there for them and support them will forever be one of my most cherished memories with teaching.

A couple of years later, the mom of one of these kiddos reached out to me. She wanted to thank me for listening to her son and providing information that he readily shared with people in his community. She said that he had never had a connection with a teacher like he had with me. He trusted me and knew that I was looking out for him and his family.

—TYLER, SPECIAL EDUCATION TEACHER

Share which videos were most impactful to you and to your students. We are so eager to hear which ones resonated strongly. Be sure to tag us. **#TEACHABLES**

> *The reason I'm here today is because a teacher that cared reached out and managed to tap into my soul.*
>
> — Dr. Victor Rios, educator and author

1.9 Please, Come In: Welcome Families into Your Classroom

Parental involvement is a clear predictor of educational success. According to Lily Eskelsen García and Otha Thornton's blog, "Ongoing research shows that family engagement in schools improves student achievement, reduces absenteeism, and restores parents' confidence in their children's education. Students with involved parents or other caregivers earn higher grades and test scores, have better social skills, and show improved behavior."[4] According to Cori Brewster and Jennifer Fager in the Northwest Regional Educational Laboratory booklet, they concur, adding that "active parent involvement has been associated with numerous benefits for students, including increasing student motivation and engagement in school."[5]

Parents and guardians know their children better than anyone else, and their involvement plays a crucial role in academic success. Welcome the opportunity to invite parents and guardians into the classroom, communicate with them in multiple ways, and encourage

---

4 Lily Eskelsen García and Otha Thornton, "The Enduring Importance of Parental Involvement," *National Education Association* (November 18, 2014).

5 Cori Brewster and Jennifer Fager, "Increasing Student Engagement and Motivation: From Time-on-Task to Homework," *Northwest Regional Educational Laboratory* (October 2000).

them to become engaged in their child's education. Clearly convey that educational success is a team effort between you, the student, and the parent or guardian.

Recommendations

- Extend an open invitation to parents and guardians to observe your classroom. As always, set up guidelines that ensure security and that meet the needs of your classroom and the school.
- Provide information to parents and guardians on when and how to contact you. It's important for families to respect your personal time, so encourage them to reach out to you during designated office hours or via email. Let families know you are readily available to provide support and can be contacted through these channels, ensuring smooth and effective communication.
- Have students write a letter or make a present to give to their parents or guardians at a "back-to-school night" event. If a student's parents or guardians can't attend, have the student take the gift home the next day.
- Invite parents and guardians to class to be guest speakers on a specific topic. (See the "Who's the Expert?" strategy located in section 3.5.)
- Platforms such as Remind, ClassDojo, and Infinite Campus are great ways for teachers to communicate with parents. They provide a convenient and efficient means of sharing important information, updates, and progress reports, building better parent-teacher collaboration and involvement in a student's education.
- During the first month of school, call or email each of your students' parents and guardians and provide some form of positive recognition. This might take a while to complete, but it will go a long way in building a positive connection! (See

the "Communicate, Communicate, Communicate" strategy found in section 1.4 for additional recommendations regarding parent engagement.)

- Create a survey to solicit information from parents and guardians. Sample questions could include "What are three things your child likes to do?" and "What are they interested in?" and "Is there anything that will help improve their learning environment?" and "How does your child learn best?" (See the "Communicate, Communicate, Communicate" strategy in section 1.4 on ways to disseminate the survey.)

Above and Beyond

- Explore the free Choose Love Movement, a character development and SEL program designed for pre-K through twelfth-grade students. This initiative instructs educators and students on how to choose love in any situation. The program uses simple yet powerful themes and activities for the classroom, to foster a culture where students feel safe, cared for, connected, and empowered. The program was inspired by six-year-old Jesse Lewis, hero and Sandy Hook victim.
- Watch the two-minute "Parent Involvement Makes a Difference to School Kids" video from PTO Today. Share this video with parents and guardians to help them understand the power of parental involvement and to give them tips on how they can get involved.

Inviting students' families into the classroom creates a strong partnership between teachers and parents. It allows parents to understand the classroom environment, curriculum, and teacher's expectations, which will help them to participate in their child's education and reinforce learning at home.

On social media, please share with us the different ways you connect school and home. We want to continue to provide more ideas for teachers who are looking for ways to build stronger relationships. **#TEACHABLES**

> *Every child deserves a champion, an adult who will never give up on them, who understands the power of connection and insists they become the best they can be.*
>
> — DR. RITA PIERSON, EDUCATOR

1.10 Quality Time: Make Time for Students

We know that students' relationships with their educators have important and long-lasting implications for academic and social development. According to researchers Bridget K. Hamre and Robert C. Pianta, "Having teachers who attend to their social and emotional needs may be as or more important to [students'] academic development than specific instructional practices."[6] Students who have close, positive, and supportive relationships with their teachers will attain higher levels of achievement than those without that strong bond.

The piece we often leave out of this relational equation is the positive impact a *student's* presence can have on a *teacher's* life. Most teachers choose their career because of their genuine care and desire to make a positive impact on their students. Remember to be present when you create those quality moments. The impact students have on you will last a lifetime. Cherish the opportunities.

---

6   Bridget K. Hamre and Robert C. Pianta, "Can Instructional and Emotional Support in the First-Grade Classroom Make a Difference for Children at Risk of School Failure?," *Child Development* 76, no. 5 (September 2005): 949–967.

Recommendations

- Create special time with each student. You could eat lunch together, hold a three-minute meeting, or try a 2x10 strategy (a one-on-one conversation with an at-risk student that lasts two minutes each day for ten days). Be sure to keep track so you get quality time with *all* your students.
- Make eye contact and fully concentrate on the student when having a conversation.
- Talk with your student by asking open-ended questions and applying wait time.
- Have your students use this writing activity prompt: "I wish my teacher knew . . ." Remind them that what they write is for your eyes only and you will use it to do all you can to help them with their learning. (See the "Walk in My Shoes" strategy in section 1.8.)
- Open your classroom up before and/or after school to create a safe and welcoming environment for students. Always check your school's policy on students being in your classroom during unauthorized times.
- Keep the following in mind when you're looking for areas to casually connect with students:
    - Outdoor seating areas such as benches, picnic tables, or patio furniture in school courtyards or gardens provide a place to talk with students.
    - Cafeterias or lunchrooms are convenient because students often gather in these spaces during break times, providing an opportunity for casual conversations.
    - Libraries sometimes have designated areas where students can talk quietly, allowing for more relaxed conversations.
    - Common areas such as hallways, staircases, or open spaces where students frequently pass through or hang out may provide opportunities for a conversation.

- ○ Sports fields or courts allow you to encourage conversations during physical activities like walking, jogging, or shooting hoops.
- ○ Art or music rooms can inspire creative discussions and provide a more relaxed atmosphere.
- Make a list of your students and write at least one thing you know about each student's life outside of school. If you struggle to come up with one thing, then it's time to get to know that student a little better.
- Take students outside and do some lessons in the fresh air. Mingle and chat with them as they work. It just feels different outside the classroom.
- Engage in a reflective exercise by prompting students to explore the profound influence of an individual in their lives. Then, have students write about that person. As they write, encourage students to delve into the intricate dynamics of the relationship they share with this person, understanding how it has played a pivotal role in shaping their personal growth and development. By examining these narratives, students gain a deeper appreciation for the transformative power of human connections, recognizing the profound impact that interpersonal bonds can have on their own identities and life trajectories.
- Have a daily classroom meeting. If you teach middle school or high school students, spend the last three to five minutes of each class period talking about events going on at the school, in the community, and globally. This strategy is a great way to maintain awareness of your classroom environment and keep relationships strong. With primary and younger students, this is a great way to start the day.

Above and Beyond

- Check out an excellent four-minute video from Edutopia, "The Power of Relationships in Schools." It will show you subtle ways to connect with your students. The video offers valuable strategies and techniques to nurture connections with students of all ages, ensuring they feel safe and supported within the educational environment. By incorporating the concepts highlighted in this video, educators can enhance their ability to form meaningful relationships with students.

- Take time for your own reflections too. Write about a person who has had an impact on your life and consider why. Writing about this specific person allows you to reflect on the significant relationships and experiences that have shaped you. It provides an opportunity to gain a deeper understanding of the ways in which they influenced your personal growth, values, and perspectives. Additionally, it serves as an expression of gratitude and appreciation, allowing you to acknowledge and honor the contributions and support you have received from that person.

- Attend extracurricular events where students are performing. This provides a valuable opportunity to find inspiration, foster community, experience other cultures, and ignite personal growth. By witnessing the dedication and hard work of students in various fields, you can gain a deeper appreciation for their skills and talents, motivating you to explore your own passions and strive for excellence. These events also create a sense of community and provide relationship-building opportunities.

This letter was written by a student who completed the "I wish my teacher knew . . ." activity.

> I wish my teachers knew that out of all the teachers here there are only three that I feel are the most understandable. These three teachers are Mrs. C, Ms. M, and Ms. P. They are really comprehensive of students and are patient with us. They are also teachers who will support you through anything you are going through; either at home or in school. Thank you for working at our school and being the best teachers.
>
> **—ROSA, FOURTH GRADER, COLORADO**

On social media, share some of your students' responses to the "I wish my teacher knew . . ." prompt. (Withhold their names but include their grade level.) Be sure to tag us! **#TEACHABLES**

> *What the science of learning and development tells us is that we need to create learning environments, which allow for strong, long-term relationships for children to become attached to school and to the adults and other children in it.*
>
> — DR. LINDA DARLING-HAMMOND, PRESIDENT AND CEO OF LEARNING POLICY INSTITUTE

1.11 Positive Language: Choose Your Words Thoughtfully

There are many studies that show how many positive messages are needed to offset a negative one.

The praise-to-criticism ratio is anywhere from two to six, but really the specific number doesn't matter. What *does* matter is knowing it takes at least double the number of positive comments to balance out the negative.

You don't have control over what students are hearing at home, but in your classroom you can provide an environment where negative language is not acceptable. Will there be slipups? You bet there will be. But if the language is corrected and the *why* is provided, adopting more positive phrasing can make a real impact. Positive language encourages positive behavior, builds positive relationships, and makes the overall classroom environment—you guessed it—positive!

Recommendations

- As a class, discuss what negative and positive language means. Ask your students to come up with positive language statements. Once you have your list, ask them to create posters (this works for all grade levels and content areas). Hang the posters around your classroom as a reminder to use positive language when redirecting someone or stopping a specific behavior.
- Manage behavior positively and proactively by implementing strategies and techniques that promote positive behavior and prevent challenging or disruptive behaviors. This will require you to be flexible, consistent, and patient. Here are some ideas to get you started:
    - Create an environment that is supportive, nurturing, and inclusive.
    - Communicate your expectations and rules concerning appropriate behavior. You also need to make it clear what consequences will occur if there is inappropriate behavior.

- Teach and model appropriate behavior and reinforce the positive behavior by recognizing it and providing specific praise.
  - Teach students techniques such as deep breathing exercises or using a calm-down corner to help them with self-regulation.
- The next time you need to redirect or stop specific behavior, try one of the positive language approaches below:

Instead of . . .	Try . . .
Be quiet!	Softer voices, please.
This is a big mess.	Let's keep our space neat and organized.
Don't cry.	It's OK to cry.
Do you have any questions?	What questions do you have?
We did this yesterday.	Let's try a quick refresh.
You're OK.	How are you doing?
You need to listen.	I want to help you.
Don't say that!	Please use kind words.
Do you need help?	I can help if you need me.
Don't give up.	Keep going, you're making progress.
You're wrong.	Let's explore a different perspective.
Don't be disrespectful.	Let's treat each other with respect.
Stop talking!	It's important to maintain silence.
Do you need help?	I'm here if you need assistance.
You need to listen.	I want to make sure you understand.

- Create a cheat sheet of sentence stems that can be used to redirect a negative behavior that continues to occur in your classroom. Remember, the tone and context in which these phrases are used are crucial. It's important to approach students with respect, empathy, and a willingness to help them learn and grow. Here are a few examples:

- ° "It looks like . . ." (Example: "It looks like you two both want to use the red paint. I'll give each of you some.")
- ° "I like seeing . . ." (Example: "I like seeing that you are excited about this project, but we need to bring the volume down just a bit so we don't disturb the other classes.")
- ° "I know you are excited about . . ." (Example: "I know you are excited about getting to lunch, but let's slow down so we don't run into anyone.")

Above and Beyond

- Watch the three-minute video by Fearless Soul on YouTube called "Teacher Makes Shocking Error but His Response is Priceless." It's about a teacher who made a mistake and his response to his students when they laughed at him. Share this video with your students if appropriate.

For years, I crafted colorful notes to slip into my children's lunch boxes, adorned with stamped images and heartfelt messages. Little did I know that one day, a note from one of my child's friends would find its way back to me, brightening my world in return.

Hey Tyler's Mom. It's low key super cute that you send a note every day with Tyler's lunch. I thought you deserved to get a note too.

—ALLIE, ELEVENTH GRADER, COLORADO

Please share with us on social media how shifting your words toward positivity has made a difference in your class-room. Please tag us. **#TEACHABLES**

> *Be the person who encourages others, who chooses to see the good in the world and speak it out loud. Be frequent in your praise and thoughtful in your criticism.*
>
> — SOUL STORIES BY FEARLESS SOUL

Story: The Power of Connections

If I had to provide one word to sum up what is needed for a success-ful educational career, it would have to be relationships! Regardless of whether someone is just starting school to become a teacher, is new to teaching, or is a veteran teacher, their relationships are foundational. You could have the perfect classroom, the most prepared lessons, and a doctorate in educational theories, but if you don't know how to build relationships with students, then you will never help your students reach their highest level of achievement.

There is so much truth in this phrase: "Students don't care how much you know until they know how much you care." Students are some of the best judges of character: they pick up on our cues, tone, body language, and intent. So very often I have had young adults call me by name in stores, restaurants, airports, and conferences. I didn't teach these students, but they certainly remembered me. They often have a story of how I always said hello to them in the hall, how I made them happy at recess, or how I spent time with them on a field trip. "We all wanted to be in your classroom" is a phrase that still brings me joy, but now that I'm in lots of classrooms every day, it makes my heart hurt a little. Why can't every teacher create an environment that students want to be a part of?

I've lived in Colorado for almost twenty years now, and I have seen a lot of my fourth, fifth, and sixth graders grow into amazing adults. We catch up over coffee, lunch, or dinner, and 100 percent of the time, they recall a moment when I made their not-so-great day better by simply stopping to listen, showing I cared, or asking how they were. Something else they often say is how I was vulnerable. You see, I shared when I was having a bad day or when their behaviors impacted me. I also simply apologized if I had lost my patience the day or hour before.

Thanks to social media, the students I taught in other states have reached out to share the difference I made in their lives by not giving up on them, by staying in at recess to listen, by staying after school to help them with something they weren't mastering, or by teaching a life skill that they use all the time as an adult. I can't explain the pure joy I feel when I receive one of these special messages. Here's one from a young man who was not the easiest boy to teach. He often had troubles with other students at recess, in music class, in PE, and on the bus. I would have never thought in a million years that he would think of me when he was an adult, but he did.

> The best teacher ever! Hey, Ms. Abla I don't know if you remember me but you were my fourth grade teacher when I moved to Colorado. Just wanted to say hi and let you know I've always thought of you as the best and most awesome nicest teacher I've ever had. I still remember the first day I showed up I was freaking out but you made it easier to adapt. Till this day no teacher or elder has shown me the kindness you did. I just want to say thank you for everything you did for me. When I get depressed and sad and I'm about to give up on people I think back and remember the kindness you showed me. It's gotten me out of some bad times. I just want to say thank you for everything.

P.S. I have a 10 month old son now. I hope he can have a teacher like you when he grows up.

—LIAM, FORMER FOURTH-GRADE STUDENT, COLORADO

No matter how much English a language learner speaks upon arriving at school, and no matter how much of their native language the educator speaks, a smile transcends all.

JANE HILL, EDUCATOR AND AUTHOR

Chapter 2

Organization and Procedures

FROM THE VERY FIRST DAY WITH YOUR STUDENTS, BUILDING RELATIONSHIPS IS A MUST. Right behind that comes organization and procedures. These will guide the learning process and save valuable teaching minutes, enhancing classroom success. When students know your expectations, it becomes much easier for them to focus on learning.

Reflect on a time when you entered a meeting or conference and there was no one at the door to welcome you, provide an agenda, or explain the goal of the gathering or presentation. Didn't you feel your anxiety creep in as you looked around for a familiar face or protocol to provide needed structure and direction? Our students are no different. To eliminate uncertainty, be purposeful in creating structures and procedures that will reduce variability and create a safe learning environment.

A classroom without structure might work for a time, but you need organization and procedures in the long run. Demonstrations of care need to be matched by organizational methods. When we take the time to teach students procedural norms, the classroom becomes a well-oiled machine that can practically run itself. Having the classroom organized and ready for rigorous learning shows students that you care about *what* you are teaching and *who* you are teaching.

When it comes to setting expectations for classroom processes, model, practice, model, and practice again. This way, everyone will have a clear understanding of what is expected from the moment they walk in the classroom door until the minute they leave the room. Students also need to be reminded of the rules and expectations occasionally—and always after any type of school break.

Let's not forget about expectations for ourselves either. While you're teaching, you need to be up and circulating throughout the classroom, facilitating learning and checking for understanding. You should be on your feet interacting with your students for most of the school day unless you're working with a small group or watching a spectacular presentation of your students' teaching. Active teaching is just as important as active learning.

As you consider how best to tackle strategies for organization and procedures, look at your classroom and quiz yourself about possible points of confusion for students—and how you might head them off.

Q: Do my students like sitting at desks in rows?

A: I can survey them to find out their preferences and try to accommodate everyone. (See the "Getting to Know You" and "A Different Look" strategies in sections 1.3 and 2.7, respectively.)

Q: What kind of music should I play as students enter the classroom?

A: I can ask them to provide me with their favorite (appropriate) songs and create a playlist. (See the "Getting to Know You" and "Play the Music" strategies in sections 1.3 and 3.10, respectively.)

Q: Are all my posters of old guys from a hundred years ago?

A: I can find or create posters that help my students see connections between themselves and contemporary successful people.

(See the "Where in the World?" and "A Different Look" strategies in sections 1.7 and 2.7, respectively.)

Q: If a student forgets a pencil, where can they find a sharpened one to use?

A: On the first day of class, I'll tell students where they can find extra materials, and I'll periodically remind them. (See the "This Is How We Roll" strategy found in section 2.1.)

Q: Does everybody like all the walls being covered with posters?

A: Students can help me decorate the classroom and make changes every now and then. (See the "A Different Look" and "Working Walls" strategies in sections 2.7 and 4.4, respectively.)

Q: Am I going to require students to raise their hand and announce to the whole class when they need to go to the restroom?

A: I'll provide the processes for students going to the restroom on the first day of class, and I'll periodically remind them. (See the "This Is How We Roll" strategy in section 2.1.)

Q: Would students benefit from posted learning targets that tell them what they are responsible for learning?

A: I will post learning targets every day, in the same place. (See the "I Can . . ." strategy in section 2.5.)

Q: Will the students and I like one another?

A: I will start building relationships with each student from day one. (See the "Relationships" strategies in chapter 1.)

Q: Are the students hoping for a fun and engaging year? Will it be one?

A: Yes and yes! (See any of the strategies.)

Every bit of time and effort you put into making your classroom environment the best it can be will matter!

Above and Beyond

We've designed comprehensive checklists for elementary and secondary levels to enhance your learning environment, and we carefully crafted step-by-step instructions, with detailed descriptions, to ensure you have everything you need to create an optimal space for your educational journey. From organizing your study area to optimizing digital tools, these checklists are your go-to resource for setting up a classroom that fosters productivity, focus, and motivation.

> *Organization in the classroom is one of the best teaching practices that can make for a successful educator and class.*
>
> — OLIVIA WANNARKA, AUTHOR

Preparing for Organization and Procedures

When routines, organization, and procedures are carefully taught, modeled, and established in the classroom, students quickly learn what's expected of them. Having predictable and thorough norms in place allows teachers to spend more time on what matters most. However, there are times when something takes attention and energy away from your teaching and the students' learning (e.g., restroom breaks, drinks, announcements, sharpening of pencils, homework not completed, calling out, no one responding). When these distractions happen, you need to look at the problem and determine how to fix it so you aren't losing those precious minutes of instruction.

Here's an example of the process for determining what is detracting from focus in the classroom and for working through it to get to a solution.

What: My students are continually asking to get a drink or go to the restroom after lunch, and it becomes a revolving door with no one paying attention to my lesson or focusing on the activity.

Why: Let's first figure out why this behavior is happening. That way, you can determine what you do and do not have control over.

How: Create a list of possible solutions.

- What if we take five minutes at the start of class for everyone to grab a drink, go to the restroom, and line up outside my door?
- Is the behavior occurring because students are just coming from lunch and recess and they're thirsty?
- Could students take a restroom break during their lunch period?
- What if I'm vulnerable and tell students their behavior makes me feel unvalued? What if I tell them I'm worried they'll miss important skills because they aren't focusing 100 percent on their learning—or even thinking about the content?
- Could I have students brainstorm solutions in small groups?
- Is it always the same seven students who leave for the restroom, or is it different students each day?

Fix it: Review the possible solutions and choose one to implement. Give it one week and then determine if it improved the problem. If it did, excellent! If not, try something different from the list.

Now that you see the process, take a few minutes to reflect on the school day.

1. Use the space below to make a list of anything that gets in the way of your teaching and students' learning.

2. Choose one of the problems from your list.

3. Determine the why and how.

4. Fix it by implementing one of the possible solutions. Check in with yourself a week later to evaluate whether the solution is working.

As a reminder, you don't have to do this alone. Reach out to colleagues for advice and possible solutions. Slowly tackle one problem at a time, working methodically through each item on your list. Don't let the problem steal your joy or become a nuisance, and certainly don't ignore it. Remember, as a teacher, you have the incredible ability to make a positive impact on your students' lives. With the support of your colleagues and a determined mindset, you can conquer any obstacles and continue to inspire and shape young minds.

> *Classroom management consists of the practices and procedures that a teacher uses to maintain an environment in which instruction and learning can occur.*
>
> — HARRY K. WONG AND ROSEMARY T. WONG,
> EDUCATORS AND AUTHORS

2.1 This Is How We Roll: Smooth Processes and Procedures

From a very early age, we are taught rules and procedures that are modeled and reinforced: getting up when the alarm goes off (hitting the snooze button only a couple of times), brushing and flossing (at least occasionally) before going to bed, and looking both ways before crossing the street.

Rules and procedures are all around us every day, and the situation is no different in the classroom. Having rules and procedures helps to create a learning environment that is safe, positive, and engaging. Many teachers struggle with classroom management because it can seem overwhelming, but it doesn't have to be if you communicate expectations to your students and if you model, practice, reinforce, and occasionally review the rules and procedures.

Establishing Norms—Together

Involve students in creating a class motto and four to six classroom expectations. Making this a collaborative process will foster a sense of ownership, responsibility, and engagement within the classroom community. This activity will look different based on the age you teach, so adapt it to best meet the needs of your students. This process might take anywhere from one to two hours, depending on how deep you go. You can space this over several days or class periods, but the investment of time will pay off throughout the school year. This is a great activity to get students communicating, collaborating, and compromising. Here are steps to help get you started:

1. Begin by explaining that it's important to have a class motto and classroom expectations because this helps create a positive learning environment for everyone in the classroom.

2. Provide an opportunity for your students to share their thoughts and ideas regarding appropriate behavior in school. Encourage them to think about values such as fairness, inclusivity, positivity, kindness, compassion, cooperation, and courage.

3. Once you have a comprehensive list of ideas, have your students form small groups. Assign each group a specific behavior to discuss and have them work to create clear and concise statements.

4. After the group discussions, have each group present their statement to the class. Encourage everyone to discuss the statements and provide feedback. Remind students that as a

class you'll need to narrow the expectations down to a maximum of six. See if students can find a way to combine some of the statements.

5. After classroom expectations are finalized, the class will need to create a short class motto that is meaningful and easy to remember.

6. Upon completion, have your students create a visual product that will be prominently displayed in the classroom. Throughout the year, refer to the motto to reinforce and remind everyone of the agreed-upon expectations and overall class motto.

7. You can also have students sign their name on the class motto as a form of signing a yearlong school contract.

Recommendations

- Post classroom expectations and procedures in a prominent place and refer to them periodically, not just when one is being broken. When possible, have students sign an agreement.

- State expectations in positive language (avoid words such as *don't*). Rather than telling students what they shouldn't do, tell them what they can do. For example, instead of saying "Don't tap your pencil on the desk," provide them with a fidget. Instead of saying "Don't ask to go to the restroom during lecture or group activity time," say "Remember, if you have to take a restroom break, they are to be taken during independent work time." (For more examples, see the "Positive Language" strategy in section 1.11.)

- Primary and elementary students can create a short skit or video clip modeling appropriate procedures for specific tasks. Post the skits or videos on your classroom website for parents and guardians, new students, and your current class (so you can periodically review). Task examples include:

- ○ How to indicate lunch choices
- ○ How and where to turn in homework
- ○ Procedures for bell work
- ○ How to ask questions during class
- ○ Process for completing assignments after being absent
- ○ Procedures to follow for a restroom break
- ○ Process for leaving the classroom
- ○ How to access classroom supplies
- ○ Snack time procedures
- ○ Recess procedures
- ○ Expectations for hallway behavior
- ○ How to enter the classroom

- Set a class goal of earning extra recess, free time, and/or game time. Award points or put stones in a jar (adding, not removing) as the procedures are performed by a specific student or the class. This recommendation promotes collective efficacy within a classroom community. (See the "Caught Ya" strategy in section 1.2 for directions.)
- Ask for help in setting expectations! Reach out to a colleague for advice and recommendations. Consistency among classrooms will help your students and reduce variability from classroom to classroom. Ultimately, consistency helps create a cohesive and equitable learning environment for students across different classrooms.

Above and Beyond

- View the eighteen-minute "My Daily Classroom Management Strategies" video by Real Rap with Reynolds to hear about some of his daily procedures and practices.
- Review the Edutopia article "New Teachers: Fundamentals of Classroom Management" to get a ton of resources for developing routines, fostering classroom community, managing

disruptions, and building student relationships from pre-K through twelfth grade.

The simplicity of a stone jar, coupled with competition and participation among students, can remarkably uplift the classroom atmosphere and create a significant impact. The transformative power of these elements should not be under-estimated. They foster engagement, motivation, and a sense of accomplishment among students.

Dear Mrs. Abla,

Thank you for being such a great teacher all the time. You let us learn freely and not have to do boring lessons all day. Also, thank you for making things challenging and fun to learn. I like the stone jar also because we get to do fun things all the time. Unlike most teachers at other schools, you care about us and actually try to make school not seem like a boring prison all the time. Thank you again and I wish I could be in your class more.

—ZANE, SIXTH GRADER, COLORADO

Share a copy of your classroom's motto and/or expectations on social media. Please tag us! **#TEACHABLES**

The main components of organization in the classroom are effective classroom management, creating a positive learning environment, and the physical set-up of the room.

OLIVIA WANNARKA, AUTHOR

2.2 Let's Get This Learning Started: Setting the Stage for Learning

Students are more successful when they have a relevant task to complete as they enter the classroom. Sometimes this is referred to as *bell work* or *do-now work*. Providing a daily prompt that is engaging, controversial, fun, or relevant to what students are learning creates a great opportunity to spark curiosity and get students thinking about the content you're about to teach. In a self-contained classroom, bell work helps to smooth transitions between subjects, and it primes students for the next lesson, fostering a more engaging learning environment.

We want students engaged and actively learning from the moment they walk into the classroom; however, bell work shouldn't bleed into your lesson, so be sure to set a timer for five minutes. End bell work as soon as the timer goes off and begin your lesson. By implementing bell work, educators can optimize classroom management and maximize student participation.

Recommendations

Below are examples of bell work prompts that will engage students from the moment they walk into the classroom:

- As their "entrance ticket" to class, have students solve a math problem based on the previous day's lesson.
- Have students complete a simple task that you covered the day before. Example: tell the student next to you the steps to make biscuits.
- Ask a question that will hook students and relate to the next lesson, such as "Is a pumpkin a fruit or a vegetable and why?"
- Have students draw a picture, such as the main parts of a tree.

- Ask students to complete a prompt. Examples: "Today will be a terrific day because I will . . ." or "I am grateful for . . ." or "I want to learn more about . . ."
- Have students do as many jumping jacks as they can.
- Ask a reading question, such as "What book are you currently reading and why?"
- Have students solve a riddle. Example: Why do bees hum?
  - Answer: Because they don't know the words.
- Ask students to respond to a controversial statement like "Does technology make us more alone?"
- Ask a "Would you rather . . ." question. Examples: "Would you rather run one mile or walk five miles?" or "Would you rather eat chocolate ice cream or vanilla ice cream?" or "Would you rather swim in the ocean or hike in the mountains?"
- Ask students to respond to a newsworthy event (local, national, international).
- The following songs have meaningful lyrics that help students infer the intended message of the writer. It can also be a great opportunity to incorporate Social and Emotional Learning (SEL) by discussing the lyrics. Examples:
  - "Just the Way You Are" by Bruno Mars
  - "Beautiful" by Christina Aguilera
  - "Stand by Me" by Ben E. King
  - "Survivor" by Destiny's Child
  - "Beautiful Day" by U2
  - "We Are the World" by United Support of Artists for Africa
- The following movies have memorable quotes, lessons, and provide opportunities for discussion. Have students find a quote to elaborate the meaning in their own words. Examples:
  - *Braveheart*
  - *Hidden Figures*

- *Cool Hand Luke*
- *Parasite*
- *Apollo 13*
- *Dead Poets Society*
- *La Bamba*

- Occasionally have the students share their responses to bell work, or ask them to partner up to discuss the prompt or task. This allows students to express their unique perspectives, promoting a collaborative learning environment where knowledge and ideas are exchanged. Partnering up enhances communication skills, teamwork abilities, and critical thinking. The intent is to create an interactive and inclusive atmosphere that supports learning, engagement, and the development of essential skills.

Above and Beyond

- Watch Edutopia's "60-Second Strategy: Do Now Sheets" video to understand the value of getting students to think and learn the second they walk in the door. The video also provides steps you can take to implement this type of activity in your classroom.

Creating clear, focused, and precise procedures and processes in the classroom maximizes instructional time while minimizing wasted time. When students know exactly what to do and when to do it, they can transition smoothly between activities, stay engaged, and make the most of every learning opportunity.

Please share your favorite bell work or do-now work with us on social media. **#TEACHABLES**

> *One common struggle for teachers is to promote a smooth and productive start to the day or class, which is critical to creating the initial momentum for academic engagement.*
>
> — Dr. Clayton R. Cook et al., researchers

2.3   Class Class: Quick Ways to Quiet the Class

There is a magical hum of learning in high-performing classrooms. Students need to process their learning in small groups, with partners, or through cooperative learning. However, regardless of the talking structures you implement, there comes a time when you need to pull the class together to listen. In pre-K through twelfth grade, fostering collaboration and maintaining students' attention during lessons is crucial. Teach and practice a quiet signal with your students; it will indicate when they must be silent and focus their attention fully on you. Continue to practice and model the technique until you have complete attention from all students.

After using the technique for a while, you and your students will get tired of the signal you chose. Variety is the spice of life, so choose and teach a different quiet signal. While the following list contains ideas suitable for all grades, it's important to consider your students' individual needs and preferences. Let's make learning enjoyable and interactive!

Recommendations

- Use chimes—they work like a dream! They are a calm and peaceful way to get your students' attention. Ring the chimes and watch as students raise their hands and move their fingers along with the sound.

- Raise your hand and have students raise theirs in response. Give them a maximum of five seconds to conclude their conversation and raise their hand after you have raised yours.

- Hold up five fingers and move around the room. As students notice and start to pay attention, drop to four fingers, then three, then two, then one as they all get quiet.

- Use call-and-response techniques to help redirect all students to specific procedures or next steps. Here are some examples:

Teacher	Student
One, two, three, look at me!	One, two, look at you!
Chicka, chicka	Boom, boom
Awesome!	Possum!
Hocus pocus	Everybody focus
Ready to rock?	Ready to roll!
Flat tire!	Shhhhhhhh!
Class, class	Yes, yes
One, two, three, eyes on me!	One, two, eyes on you!
Macaroni cheese	Everybody freeze
Stop	Collaborate and listen

- Use a Tibetan singing bowl to calmly quiet the class so they will be ready to listen to the next set of directions.

- Flicker the light and say, in a very upbeat voice, "Show me your listening wings!" The kids should stop what they're doing and stretch their arms out to let you know that they are listening!

- Say "Hands on top, that means stop." The kids stop what they're doing because their hands must touch the tops of their heads.
- Use a simple ringtone on your cell phone. This should be loud enough to get attention and can work as a quiet-time signal as well.
- Use a remote doorbell to focus attention. You can keep the remote with you while you're circulating the classroom during collaborative projects.
- Use a concierge bell with coded signals: one ding means the class must simmer down and be aware of the noise level, and two quick dings means the whole class's attention is needed or a transition is about to occur.
- Softly say "If you can hear me, clap once." Wait for the response and then say "If you can hear me, clap twice."
- Teach students to respond to a verbal call by mimicking it to show attention. For example, if you say "Claaaaaaaassss," they respond "Yeeessssssss?" Make it fun by switching it up—you could use a southern drawl or a British accent.

Above and Beyond

- "Demonstrating Self-Regulation with Tone of Voice" is a two-minute video that shows when teachers model self-regulation by using a voice that is calm, neutral, and assertive, they help students feel cared for—and ready to learn. Please take note that although the video showcases elementary students, its content is relevant and applicable to students from pre-K to twelfth grade.

Encouraging active discussions and information processing among students is vital in learning environments, but so is a quiet signal that allows for seamless redirection and

> transitions. There is a pleasant blend of teacher and student talk that supports an environment where learning flows and students remain engaged.

On social media, share the quiet signal from the "Class Class" strategy that you use in your classroom. Please also share other quiet signals you use to bring your students back together. And tag us! **#TEACHABLES**

> *Achieve starts with believe! Sometimes a positive word or two changes a life for scholars in waiting.*
>
> — RITA WIRTZ, EDUCATOR AND AUTHOR

2.4 Lifelong Skills: Teach Soft Skills

It's crucial that students develop desirable and suitable conduct, characteristics, qualities, and skills. These will play a significant role in their life. Having strong soft skills—such as communication, adaptability, and teamwork—improves academic performance because these social skills make students resilient and able to take feedback and relate to others. This will benefit students in their education and future employment. You can help students build soft skills by modeling and practicing when the opportunity arises.

Making Time for Time Management Skills

Help students practice time management by giving them a task and asking them to determine how long they think it will take to complete. They should estimate the time, complete the task, and then check their estimation versus the final time.

Start small. For example, ask students how long it takes them to do ten push-ups or how long it takes them to get up, sharpen a pencil, and sit back down. Then increase the time and the length of the task. For example, have students write a six-sentence paragraph or find the definition of five vocabulary terms and then write those definitions in their own words. By focusing on three steps—setting priorities, creating schedules, and managing distractions—students can develop a solid foundation in time management that can benefit them academically and as adults.

Here are some other ideas for fostering time management skills:

- Help students understand the importance of setting priorities. Teach them how to identify their most important tasks or goals and rank them based on urgency and importance. Encourage students to focus on high-priority tasks first to ensure they allocate their time and energy effectively.
- Guide students in creating schedules or timetables to organize their time. Teach them how to break down large tasks into smaller, more manageable chunks, and tell them to allocate specific time slots for each task. Emphasize the importance of sticking to the schedule and avoiding procrastination.
- Teach students strategies for managing distractions and maintaining focus. Help them identify common distractions such as social media, phones, or noise, and discuss techniques to minimize or eliminate these distractions. Encourage students to create an environment conducive to studying and to set boundaries with technology and interruptions to optimize their concentration.

Building Emotional Intelligence

By teaching emotional intelligence, you can help students develop essential skills for understanding and managing their emotions, relating to others empathetically, and creating healthy and harmonious relationships. These skills are beneficial in personal, social, and professional aspects of life, leading to improved well-being. Here's some information to get you started.

Identifying emotions:

- Why: Understanding and recognizing emotions helps students gain self-awareness, enhances their ability to manage their emotions, and improves their understanding of others.
- How:
  - Encourage self-reflection through journaling or mindfulness exercises.
  - Provide resources, such as emotion charts or worksheets, to help students identify and label their emotions.
  - Use storytelling or real-life examples to illustrate the importance of emotional awareness.

Controlling emotions:

- Why: Emotional control allows students to respond effectively to challenging situations, make rational decisions, and maintain positive relationships. It reduces impulsivity and promotes overall well-being.
- How:
  - Teach various emotion regulation techniques, such as deep breathing, relaxation exercises, or cognitive reframing.
  - Practice problem-solving skills to help students address the underlying causes of their emotions and develop effective coping strategies.
  - Model emotional control in your own behavior and provide guidance on managing stress and frustration.

Showing empathy:

- Why: Empathy enhances relationships, fosters understanding, and creates a supportive and inclusive environment. It helps students connect with others, resolve conflicts, and offer support during difficult times.

- How:
  - Discuss different viewpoints to encourage students to imagine themselves in others' shoes.
  - Practice active listening skills and provide opportunities for students to share their feelings and experiences.
  - Engage in empathy-building activities, such as role-playing or group discussions, to deepen understanding and empathy.

Communicating feelings effectively:

- Why: Effective communication of emotions promotes understanding, prevents misunderstandings, and builds stronger relationships. It allows students to express their needs, boundaries, and concerns authentically.
- How:
  - Teach assertive communication techniques, such as using "I" statements and active listening.
  - Provide examples and scenarios for students to practice expressing their emotions assertively.
  - Encourage a safe and nonjudgmental environment where students feel comfortable sharing their feelings.

Appreciating people's uniqueness:

- Why: Valuing diversity promotes inclusivity, respect, and a sense of belonging. Appreciating people's uniqueness enhances empathy, encourages open-mindedness, and enriches personal growth.
- How:
  - Celebrate diversity by exploring different cultures, traditions, and perspectives.

- ◦ Encourage students to share their unique experiences and viewpoints.
- ◦ Foster a respectful and inclusive environment where everyone's contributions are valued and appreciated.

Recommendations

- Use a small hula hoop and demonstrate the invisible personal space around each person. This will help students understand boundaries.
- Model and practice a "just-right" handshake that is firm and accompanied by eye contact and a sincere smile. Remind your students that this is important because it conveys confidence and respect, establishing a positive connection with the person you're greeting.
- Model and practice what an engaged listener looks like in a conversation. By understanding and embodying the qualities of an engaged listener, students can develop empathy, build stronger relationships, and effectively collaborate with their peers, preparing them for success in both academic and professional settings.
- Teach students that mindfulness is particularly important when they are stressed and angry, as it equips them with essential tools to manage their emotions, fostering a calm and focused learning environment. By cultivating mindfulness, students develop self-awareness and self-regulation skills, enabling them to make more intentional choices. This can help them to handle conflicts constructively and improve their overall emotional well-being, which enhances their academic performance and personal growth.
- Practice relaxation techniques like deep breathing and mindfulness meditation with your students. This can activate the body's relaxation response, reducing stress levels and

promoting a calm state of mind. Meditation helps alleviate stress and anxiety associated with high-stakes assessments, enabling students to approach these with greater clarity and focus. By incorporating meditation before assessments, students can improve their cognitive processes related to attention and concentration. Mindfulness meditation, in particular, involves focusing on the present moment, which strengthens these cognitive abilities. With increased focus, students can better engage with the assessment material, leading to improved information processing and performance.

- Learning is fun and enjoyable, so implement play. Students should see that learning entails discovery and adventure. Remember, play is not for elementary students only.

Above and Beyond

- It's easy to forget the influence you hold. In this one-minute video called "How Do Teachers Change Lives?" Edutopia asked students how teachers have changed their lives. Watch it to be reminded of the impact you make every day.

It's crucial for teachers to form genuine connections with their students. This fosters trust, creates a supportive learning environment, and enhances student engagement. When students feel valued and understood, they are more likely to actively participate in class, seek guidance, and take risks in their learning, ultimately leading to improved academic performance and overall well-being.

Mrs. Abla,

I don't know if you remember me, but I was in your third-grade class in Missouri. I now have a third grade daughter and as I dropped her off at school today I thought of you.

I hope someday that she has a teacher that makes her feel loved, seen, intelligent, worth the effort, and happy. You did all those things for our class and more.

I'm sorry I haven't reached out to you before now. I have thought about you, our class, the love you had for everyone, and how much I enjoyed coming to school because of you. I simply have not taken the time to locate you and let you know what a difference you made in my life. I am certain I am a better mom because you modeled unconditional love every day in our classroom and I have taken those values and life skills and applied them in my work, with friends, my family, and how I treat strangers.

I am an attorney in Springfield, MO and contribute my drive, hard work, and dedication to the numerous life skills lessons you shared with us in school. I am constantly staying in my hula hoop space! ☺

Thank you for making a difference in my life!

—ASH, FORMER THIRD-GRADE STUDENT, MISSOURI

On social media, share which "Lifelong Skills" strategy you recently used in your classroom. If you have others, we'd love to hear about them. Be sure to tag us. **#TEACHABLES**

Skills like effective confrontation, empathy, and patience are not soft skills. They are human skills, and they must be learned.

———— SIMON SINEK, AUTHOR AND MOTIVATIONAL SPEAKER

2.5 I Can . . . : Setting Students Up for Success with Clear Learning Targets

As a teacher, it's your job to do your best to help students learn course content. To do that, you need to clarify what your students must know, understand, and be able to do by the end of the class period. Students should never have to try and figure out what they should be learning and why they need to learn it.

Toward that end, strategies like learning targets, goals, objectives, and "I can" or SWBAT (students will be able to) statements are the best way to clarify what students need to focus on. These strategies also help students understand the relevance of lessons, their connection to the larger world, and simply the *why* of why they need to pay attention.

Recommendations

- Find a place in the classroom that is large enough to post the learning target for each subject you teach. Make it an eye-catching focal point so students can see it the minute they walk into the classroom. For example, you could use painter's tape to make boxes to write in. Look at examples of student-friendly learning targets on our website.

- Remember to use verbs when helping students understand what they'll be able to do as a result of their learning. Keep the following list handy: draw, analyze, create, build, solve, present, role-play, compare, evaluate, manipulate, and infer.

- To enhance instruction, prioritize a learning target by referencing it before, during, and after the lessons. Clearly communicate the learning target at the beginning of each lesson, ensuring students understand the intended outcome. Throughout the lesson, consistently link students' activities, discussions, and reflections to the learning target, emphasizing the relevance and purpose of their engagement. Regularly check for understanding and provide feedback that reinforces the connection between students' efforts and the learning target. Conclude the lesson by summarizing key points, facilitating reflection, and previewing future lessons that build upon the current learning target, emphasizing the continuous nature of learning.

- Have students discuss with one another what they are learning and have a couple of groups share with the whole class so you can check for understanding.

- Remember to use academic language in your posted learning targets. This means specialized vocabulary, grammar, discourse, and functional skills associated with academic instruction, materials, and tasks. Students of all ages love to sound like a mathematician, scientist, historian, or author. By providing academic language for their discussions and writing, you can foster deeper connection with the content.

- Help students replace "I can't" statements with "I will." See our "The Power of Effort" strategy in section 4.1 for ideas on how to help students make this essential change to their belief in themselves.

- Talk with your colleagues to find out what types of learning targets they use and where they post them in their classrooms. Consistency among classrooms will help your students and reduce variability.

Students like to know what's in it for them and why they need to pay attention. Why do they need to know something in particular? By posting, discussing, and referencing the learning target, you'll provide students with the context they need to understand the lesson's purpose. This results in greater student buy-in.

On social media, please share pictures of your learning targets with us. We want to see where they're posted, what they sound like, and how you use them with your students. Remember to tag us! **#TEACHABLES**

> *What you do makes a difference, and you have to decide what kind of difference you want to make.*
>
> — DR. JANE GOODALL, PRIMATOLOGIST

2.6 Phones and Tablets and Laptops, Oh My!: Using Technology Procedures to Ensure Success with Electronic Devices

Students today have grown up with technological devices in their hands. They know how to use them and aren't a bit afraid of them. As long as there are clear procedures and safety guidelines, technology can provide opportunities for students to research, learn, and create. Integrating technology successfully in your classroom will enhance students' thinking and learning while creating a student-centered environment that promotes collaboration, creativity, communication, cooperation, and higher-level thinking. If it doesn't do these things, then rethink why you are including technology.

Recommendations

- Provide clear directions and expectations for all technology devices. Model these for your students again and again. As a starting point, students should know how to do the following:
  1. Remove a device from storage
  2. Turn their device on and off

3. Log in to necessary platforms
4. Close the device during teaching time and when instructions are being given
5. Store their device when it is not in use
6. Save or locate saved items in the cloud
7. Plug in their device
8. Take and post clear images

- Have your students put their phones in silent mode and place them facedown on the corners of their desks. Students should know only to use them when asked to research something. Have strict protocols about this behavior and stick to them.

- Have parents and guardians work with students to sign a user agreement detailing the procedures and use of technology at school. This agreement is typically created by the school administration, but you can also create your own. There may be consequences if a student does not sign the agreement. These could include restricted access to school technology, limited privileges, missing out on important information, and disciplinary actions for noncompliance. It is important for everyone involved to review and sign the agreement to ensure a clear understanding of expectations and responsibilities.

- Use a video conferencing tool (e.g., Skype, Zoom, Microsoft Teams, Google Meet) to connect globally with other classrooms. You can discuss current events around the world or assign students to team up and read a novel together. (See the "Let's Explore" strategy in section 3.1, the "Have You Read This? You Have to Read This!" strategy in section 3.4, and the "Who's the Expert?" strategy in section 3.5.)

- Use an engaging tech platform like Nearpod or Kahoot! to teach students about cybersafety and digital citizenship.

- Create a secure Facebook, Instagram, and/or X (formerly known as Twitter) account to showcase student work, accomplishments, and daily learning for family members and the students themselves to see. It's also a fabulous resource for front-loading content and creating a hook to get students excited about learning. But be sure to talk with your students about cyberbullying. Let them know that you are a safe person they can talk to if they are experiencing any form of bullying.

- Today's world centers around social media. You might love it or wish it'd go away, but it's here to stay. We say leverage it and use it to your advantage. It can be a wonderful communication tool for you, your students, and your students' families, as well as a way to connect globally.

Above and Beyond

- Review the "Setting Conditions for Success: Creating Effective Responsible Use Policies for Schools" resource from the International Society for Technology in Education (ISTE). It explains how to set students, parents and guardians, and educators up for success. This is an example of an effective use policy. Adapt it to best meet the needs of your school.

Smooth technology procedures and structures are crucial in the classroom. They ensure that valuable instructional time is not wasted on technical difficulties or confusion. Clear structures enable efficient troubleshooting and support, empowering teachers to address technical issues promptly and effectively. Smooth technology integration fosters a positive and productive classroom environment, enhancing student motivation, collaboration, and digital skills.

Please share on social media a picture or idea of one process or procedure you have in place for using technology in your classroom. Please tag us. #TEACHABLES

> *Technology will never replace great teachers, but technology in the hands of a great teacher can be transformational.*
>
> — GEORGE COUROS, EDUCATOR AND AUTHOR

> *La technologie ne remplacera jamais les grands enseignants, mais la technologie entre les mains d'un grand enseignant peut être transformationnelle.*
>
> — GEORGE COUROS, ÉDUCATEUR ET AUTEUR

(We have included this quote in French [from Google Translate] to model the recommendation from the "Where in the World?" strategy in section 1.7, where we advise you to use multilingual quotes in your classroom.)

2.7 A Different Look: Change Up the Arrangement of the Classroom

Students of all grade levels crave a change in their environment. Involving them in designing the classroom can be a fun way to shake things up and add a personal touch. Rearranging furniture in your own home can be refreshing, so why not bring that sense of excitement to school? As you do this, it's crucial to provide guidelines that encourage space for collaborative discussions and ensure that the room setup promotes engagement. By embracing their ideas and perspectives, you not only enhance the learning environment, but you also build a sense of pride and responsibility among your students.

Recommendations

- Have students design desk arrangements for the classroom and then select the one that works best, or have students vote on their favorite arrangement. Give your students a choice and voice.
- If available, and if it will benefit your students' learning, implement flexible seating (e.g., beanbag chairs, cushions or mats, exercise balls, or scoop chairs).
- Showcase student work to foster a positive learning environment. Students will feel a sense of belonging in their classroom, and it's a great way to help them learn from each other. You could display writing samples (e.g., a draft next to the final version), artwork, or a mathematics equation. None of the items should have a score on them. As you rotate the items on display, it is imperative that you feature all students at some point during the chosen time frame (e.g., the month, quarter, or semester).
- Leave a section or a whole wall open and ask students what they want to do with it. Let them be creative and change it up occasionally. However, be sure to leave some wall space clear; you don't need to cover every inch. Too much can be overstimulating.
- Cover filing cabinets with colorful paper or student artwork to liven up the drab color.
- Display motivational posters. Remember to make them diverse and use multilingual quotes. (See the "Where in the World?" strategy located in section 1.7.)
- Use artificial trees and flowers or get a low-maintenance plant to bring color to your room.
- Change your classroom design at least once every semester. You don't have to change everything; subtle changes are nice too.

- Design a calming space or corner in your room. This will serve as a refuge for students of all ages to retreat and unwind when they need to regulate their emotions.
- Post positive quotes around your room. Here are some examples:
  - "Always remember that I love you, you matter, you can, and I'm proud of you."
  - "My voice matters."
  - "I make a difference."
  - "I am unique and special."

Above and Beyond

Sign up at DonorsChoose.org to get funding for your classroom. It's a quick and easy way to get the items or materials your students need without paying out of your own pocket. To sign up, visit their website and click on the Teachers tab. From there, click on the Sign Up button and follow the prompts to create an account, providing information such as your name, school, and project details. Once your account is set up, you can begin requesting materials and items.

Here is a warm note from a former student who makes a point to mention the importance of a welcoming environment.

I believe a great teacher is someone who understands that kiddos come to school for a multitude of reasons, whether that be to learn, grow as a person, refuge from family, or purely just have a warm place to be for a few hours. Regardless of why they are there, it is important that a teacher respects that reason, and does everything they can to make sure the content they are teaching is touching their lives in some way. A simple essay question could change a student's life, or learning they are good at algebra equations might let them know they are good at something. It can only take one subject, or one

> teacher, to let a student know they are valuable. And a
> good teacher will recognize that change and continue
> to influence that student with their teachings in a pos-
> itive way.
>
> —ELLEN, FORMER FOURTH-GRADE STUDENT, COLORADO

Share before and after pictures of your classroom on social media. Also, let us know how this affected the engagement and overall vibe of your classroom. Please be sure to tag us. **#TEACHABLES**

Your classroom environment speaks to your students before you utter a single word. What is your classroom saying?

— MEGAN DREDGE, EDUCATOR

2.8 Everyone? Everyone?: Fostering Engagement through How You Call on Students

You have most likely seen the clip (if not, check it out) from *Ferris Bueller's Day Off* when the teacher is lecturing and then pauses for a response. "Anyone? Anyone?" he asks before moving on. "Anyone?" he asks again. What we see is a classroom full of unengaged, bored, and sleeping students.

There are easy ways to engage students in learning that will help them retain far more information than if they were passively listening. The recommendations below will help students to understand procedures and processes during collaborative and active times in the classroom. Remember, the person doing the talking is doing the learning, and no student wants a teacher like the one from *Ferris Bueller's Day Off.*

Recommendations

- Use your class roster to call on students for responses. Check a student's name off after they've answered a question so you don't keep going back to the "Hermione" in your class.
- Write students' names on popsicle sticks and place them in a container. Pull out a random stick and ask that student to respond. Have one container for each class period you teach.
- Use sticks and spoons to keep all students collaborating and learning with one another. To do this, create sticks with five different colors and spoons numbered from one to five. Put your students in groups of three to five. Assign the group a color and have the students number off in their group. Select a stick and a spoon, and the student who has that color and number responds.
- Take a deck of playing cards and write a student's name on each card. Shuffle the deck and have a student pick a card. That card determines who answers. You can also use the deck of cards to create groups based on the suits or numbers.
- Use WheelOfNames.com to randomly choose a student to reply to a prompt or question. You simply enter your students' names, spin the wheel, and you have a winner. Additionally, the name can be removed so the same student won't get chosen again, though you don't need to share that information.

Above and Beyond

- Watch the six-minute video titled "Whole Brain Teaching, High School—the Basics." What procedures can you take away from this student-focused classroom? This incredibly engaging environment empowers teachers from pre-K through twelfth grade to incorporate simple actions that will get all students invested in learning.

- Read Cheryl's "7 Ways to Spark Engagement" Edutopia blog. Student engagement is directly tied to learning. It helps to create active participation, motivation, and critical thinking, which lead to knowledge retention. Having an engaging classroom creates a positive environment.

> As a teacher, it's disheartening when you ask a thought-provoking question and only a few students raise their hands to respond while others appear disengaged. It's important to use different techniques to keep students actively engaged and listening. Knowing that they may be called on for a response is one effective approach.

How can you be sure that your students are actively engaged? Please share with us on social media what you do to engage your students. And of course, please tag us. **#TEACHABLES**

> *A number of students verbalized that when participation is required, they prepare more, and this preparation actually increases their learning.*
>
> — DRS. ELISE J. DALLIMORE, JULIE H. HERTENSTEIN, AND MARJORIE B. PLATT, PROFESSORS

2.9 Is It Really Cooperative?: Collaboration Is Key

Collaboration prepares students for the outside world by equipping them with the ability to work in teams, problem-solve, cooperate, and communicate, which are all essential skills for success in various careers.

Cooperative learning enhances creativity, critical thinking, motivation, and innovation by promoting collective thinking. It also improves reading, writing, conceptual development in science, problem-solving in mathematics, and higher-level reasoning. In addition, it has been shown to be beneficial for students from culturally diverse backgrounds as well as those with diverse learning needs.

Recall that true cooperative learning needs to have two components: positive interdependence (working together for individual and collective benefit) and individual accountability (responsibility for one's own and the group's learning). Cooperative groups should ideally have between two and five students who work together on a question, task, or discussion.

Recommendations

Cheryl is a coauthor of *Tools for Classroom Instruction That Works*,[7] a book that includes the Interaction in an Instant tool to provide quick and easy ways to incorporate cooperative learning in every lesson, every day. Each technique from the tool takes five to ten minutes of each lesson. In this recommendation, we have listed three of the seven techniques and how to use them.

As always, teach, model, and use the different approaches consistently in each lesson. As with many things, if an approach doesn't go smoothly at first, don't give up. It takes numerous attempts for the processes to become seamless. (See the "Unpack, Engage, Teach, Process, and Check" strategy in section 4.5 for additional techniques.)

- Think-Pair-Share: With a partner, students *think* about their response to the prompt, discuss their thoughts with their *pair* partner, and *share* the responses with the class.
- Numbered Heads Together: Direct students to number themselves off in groups of four. Then, provide them with a

---

7   Harvey F. Silver, Cheryl Abla, Abigail L. Boutz, and Matthew J. Perini, *Tools for Classroom Instruction That Works: Ready-to-Use Techniques for Increasing Student Achievement* (Franklin Lakes, NJ: Thoughtful Education Press, 2018), 75–79.

question. Each student must write their response and then discuss responses as a group. To increase accountability, each member of the group must be able to answer the question. Call out a number between one and four, and the student with the called-out number in each group must respond with the group's answer.

- Talking Chips: Divide students into groups of three to five and give each student two chips (counters). Provide the students with a prompt or open-ended question. To participate in the discussion, a student must place a chip in the middle. When they run out of chips, they are not allowed to speak until all the other students have used their two chips. You may have one student per group be a timekeeper so that students don't go over their speaking time limit (e.g., one minute per chip).

- Post procedures around the room with the structures for cooperative and collaborative learning. You need to teach and model often.

- Have students help write a group contract that contains the guidelines on how to maintain a positive and collaborative group. Have each person sign it.

- At the conclusion of a collaboration activity, take two to five minutes and conduct a quick formative assessment. It's always important to check for understanding with each individual student before moving on.

- Before having students work collaboratively for the first time in your classroom, have them engage in a few rounds of thumb wrestling. Pair the students up and tell them that they will have thirty seconds to win as many rounds as they can. After the first round, have students call out how many wins they had. Give them a maximum of three rounds. See if during that time they realize that working together with their partner can get them a larger number of wins.

Above and Beyond

Watch Edutopia's "60-Second Strategy: Cooperative Learning Roles" video that explains why giving students randomly assigned roles in their group work helps ensure that they all participate. The video shows you how this type of cooperative grouping is easy to include in most daily lessons.

> Learning is fun! If you and your students aren't enjoying your-selves, then pivot and make sure to include some joyful learn-ing opportunities.

On social media, please share your favorite go-to collaboration technique that both you and your students enjoy. Be sure to tag us! **#TEACHABLES**

> *I like math and social studies because my teacher makes it fun.*
>
> — PAXTON, FOURTH GRADER, OKLAHOMA

> *Because learning occurs in shared situations, language is an important tool for appropriating other mental tools. To share a strategy, we must talk about the strategy.*
>
> — DRS. ELENA BODROVA, RESEARCHER, AND DEBORAH J. LEONG, PROFESSOR

Story: Your Belief

When you envision your classroom, do you feel it's a joyful space that both you and your students want to return to? Good organization

Teachables

and clear procedures play a vital role in this "just-right" environment because they provide structure, maximize instructional time, and create a sense of stability and predictability for students.

Having clear procedures and processes in place is crucial for a well-functioning classroom, but it is equally important to cultivate a supportive environment that recognizes the abilities and worth of all students. While it may sound cliché, your belief in a student's potential can greatly impact their progress. When someone genuinely believes in them, students are more likely to thrive and develop faster. Fostering an atmosphere where every student feels valued and supported is essential for a joyful classroom environment.

I taught in a few elementary schools that were quite small, with only a couple of teachers per grade level. I learned rather quickly that parents and guardians, school board members, and administrators notice when you have strong management and relational skills. So, how did I gain my reputation for having these?

I started by building relationships with the students in the grade level before mine. This was often done in the principal's office. I made the effort because it was likely that some of those students were going to be in my class the next school year. And at the start of every new school year, I let those students know they had a fresh start. We were going to be completing projects, trying new technologies, and going on field trips that would demand a specific type of learner. My students knew I wasn't saying that to just say it. They had been observing me and my students for a few years, after all.

As my students from third, fourth, fifth, and sixth grade went on to high school and college, their parents and guardians would text pictures and tag me on social media to tell me about their child's continued accomplishments. Many times they would say it was because their child learned the importance of a good education and hard work in my classroom. I had posters around my classrooms reminding students they were "Mrs. Abla's Stars" and that "I Believe in You." I had posters that said "Oh the Places You Will Go" and "You Can and Will Do

108

It." We read about successful people, we had hard conversations, we defined what success is and how it looks and feels different for everyone. My students took quizzes to help find out their strengths and what type of learner they were, and we always talked about our passions and what made us want to learn more.

Having clear and consistent procedures in place helps create a structured and productive learning environment. When students understand the expectations and routines within the classroom, they feel more secure and confident, enabling them to focus on their learning. Organization also facilitates smooth transitions between activities, reduces confusion, and promotes efficiency in the classroom. Effective organization and procedures can maximize instructional time and create an environment conducive to students' growth and success.

> *Everything a teacher does has implications for classroom management, including creating the setting, decorating the room, arranging the chairs, speaking to children and handling their responses, putting routines in place (and then executing, modifying, and reinstituting them), developing rules, and communicating those rules to the students.*
>
> — KATHARINA SIEBERER-NAGLER, PSYCHOLOGIST

Chapter 3

Curiosity and Engagement

CHILDREN ASK NUMEROUS QUESTIONS EVERY DAY, AND THEY ARE CONSTANTLY COMING UP WITH NEW ONES FOR ANYONE WITHIN EARSHOT. Students tend to ask all those questions you don't know the answers to right off the top of your head. Who won the first Boston Marathon? What type of brushes did Pablo Picasso use? When did Amelia Earhart go missing? Where are crayons made? Why do I burp? How are cell phones made?

Sometimes we might start to get a little frustrated with the questions, especially when we have to keep answering, "I don't know. We will have to look that up." But truly we don't want that innate characteristic of curiosity to be lost. If your students aren't curious about course content, you will end up with a classroom of disengaged kids just staring at you.

More importantly, think of all the things we wouldn't know or have if curiosity was lost. Without curious people, we wouldn't have the many inventions that have helped save lives, provide conveniences, and deliver entertainment. Maurice Hilleman developed the MMR (measles, mumps, and rubella) vaccine. Shirley Jackson's curiosity helped her to make breakthroughs in scientific research with subatomic particles, and this in turn helped others invent touch-tone phones, fiber optic cables, and other cool inventions. Ray Tomlinson developed the first email, way back in 1971. Lonnie G. Johnson gave us the Super Soaker and Guillermo González Camarena invented the first colored TV screen. Finally, a big thank-you goes out to Nancy Johnson, who invented the hand-cranked ice cream maker in 1843.

Who knew? Not us. Doesn't this list of impactful discoveries get you curious about other inventions? Think of all the ways you can help your students become more curious and engaged in their learning. There are many activities, strategies, and ideas for you to get your students involved in your content area, no matter what it is.

When students are engaged, you see them leaning forward because they're intrigued and want to know more. You hear a hum of excitement as students continue to dig deeper, share more, and discover as they go. Before you begin your lesson, ask yourself, "Is there anything in here that will make my students interested enough to listen and want to learn? Would I want to learn this? Would my family members (e.g., child, niece, nephew) find this interesting? What is the hook?"

We have all sat through a class, presentation, or staff meeting that lacked engagement. As adults, we can dismiss ourselves to the restroom to keep from falling asleep, act like we received a phone call, or whisper with our neighbor. We all have our coping tactics in those lackluster predicaments. Our students aren't as fortunate. They may get the hall pass a couple of times to go somewhere and break up the boredom, but we teachers are pretty quick to notice if it happens two days in a row. If students are asking to go to the restroom, get a drink, or sleep in your classroom . . . that's a pretty big indicator that your classroom is missing engagement. Engagement sparks excitement, passion, and the desire to learn more. Students are excited about learning; it's a teacher's responsibility to stoke the fire and keep it lit. Easier said than done at times, but when done correctly it's magical!

Throughout this chapter we will provide you with numerous strategies to keep your students wide eyed, joyful, and eager for every minute of your lesson. The rest is up to you and what you do with the recommendations.

Above and Beyond
Watch Sir Ken Robinson's eighteen-minute TED talk, "Do Schools Kill Creativity?" It's sure to entertain you as you ponder that question.

> Every one of our students can learn curiosity thinking skills that will benefit their academic learning.
> — DR. JOHN MUNRO, EDUCATOR AND PSYCHOLOGIST

Preparing for Curiosity and Engagement
We know you're eager to get to the strategies, but first stop here and complete this activity to gain insights into your current practices while identifying opportunities to regularly build curiosity and engagement in your classroom.

Take five to ten minutes to sit in a quiet and comfortable space where you can reflect without distractions. Start by considering the concept of curiosity. Reflect on the following questions and write down your thoughts:

1. How often do you encourage your students to ask questions and explore topics further?
2. How do you actively seek out new knowledge and stay updated on the subjects you teach?
3. How do you encourage your students to think critically?
4. How do you create opportunities for hands-on learning, innovation, and experimentation?

Now, shift your focus to engagement. Ponder the following questions and write down your thoughts:

1. How often do you include interactive activities and discussions in your class lessons?
2. How do you create a positive and inclusive learning environment that encourages student participation?
3. Are you aware of your students' interests, strengths, and challenges, and how do you tailor your instruction based on each class's strengths and needs?
4. How do you use a variety of teaching strategies and resources to capture your students' attention and maintain their engagement?

Review your responses and consider the balance between curiosity and engagement in your daily teaching:

1. Where do you feel you could improve?
2. What specific strategies or techniques could you implement to enhance these aspects?

Set goals for yourself based on your reflections. After looking through the strategies in this chapter, identify one or two actionable steps you can take to increase curiosity and engagement in your classroom. These could be small changes or larger endeavors depending on your class and comfort level.

Implement your identified strategies or techniques in upcoming lessons. Take note of any changes you observe in student curiosity and engagement levels, as well as your own.

> *Your education and imagination will carry you to places which you won't believe possible.*
>
> — ELLISON S. ONIZUKA, ASTRONAUT

> *Na kāu hoʻonaʻauao a me kou noʻonoʻo e lawe iā ʻoe i nā wahi āu e manaʻoʻiʻo ʻole ai.*
>
> — ELLISON S. ONIZUKA, KAʻAHELE

(We have included this quote in Hawaiian [from Google Translate] to model the recommendation from the "Where in the World?" strategy in section 1.7, where we advise you to use multilingual quotes in your classroom.)

3.1 Let's Explore: Learn Anywhere

Learning can become exciting for students and teachers when it moves beyond the four walls of the classroom. A different environment can further curiosity and engagement. Remember field trips when you were a student and the impact they had on you? Collaboration is in the air as learning takes place in real time. Today's world is exciting and always changing with new technologies and inventions, so who wouldn't want to be out in it?

As a class, you can take a trip to a historical site, museum, or park. If that's just not possible, then take advantage of today's technology to go on a virtual field trip or bring the field trip to your classroom.

Creating with Green Screens

The hallways are wonderful places for your students to create movies, advertisements, or newscasts using green screens. They can conduct interviews, teach classmates about a topic, explore a location, or create an informational skit. Having students use green screens is wonderful for inquiry-based learning. They will be able to conduct research and make real-world connections. Then they'll get to engage in high-level questions and problem-solving activities while creating an educational and informative video. They can collaborate and creatively include your content area, whatever it may be, as well as reading, writing, drawing, painting, and acting. Students of all age levels can create dynamic videos using green screens.

Here is the basic process for using green screens and creating the final product:

1. Determine how much time you will spend on this project. You will need to give your students adequate time to plan, collaborate, and then design the project they will create.

2. Model the process and provide a video for students to view, or have your students model the process so others can learn from them. Have fun with your video and perhaps invite colleagues to get involved.

3. When it's time for students to start filming, you can make a green screen by purchasing a green tablecloth, cheap green material, green butcher paper, or even taping together green construction paper depending on how big you need your screen to be.

4. You can use free apps—such as PowerDirector, Chromavid, Green Screen by Do Ink, iMovie, InShot, and Filmora—to create videos. Depending on the age of your students, they could investigate and test which app will work the best for their needs.

Recommendations

- Move your learning outside. The outdoors is a haven for creative writing thoughts, exploration, mindfulness, and the pure joy of fresh air and sunshine. We all like and need a change of scenery sometimes, and this is a great way to increase engagement.

- Consider working in your school library. Libraries can provide the "just-right" space for research, small-group work, and quiet studying.

- Remember that the cafeteria is fabulous for project work. It has a tile floor and large tables for big materials.
- Try turning your classroom into a movie theater. Documentaries (e.g., *Chasing Ice* and *Planet Earth*) are a great resource to use when leaving the classroom isn't an option. Let your students sit on the floor or move desks and chairs so the classroom feels like a different environment. Have them bring snacks in to eat while they are "going to the movies."
- Bring the field trip to you. Virtual field trips are another way to increase engagement and get your students curious about their learning. Discovery Education has an extensive list of free virtual field trips categorized by subject that you can explore. Each one also has a companion guide with standards-aligned, hands-on learning activities. Go to our website to get started exploring.
- Invite experts into your classroom to have an in-school field trip. (See the "Who's the Expert?" strategy located in section 3.5 for more information.)

Above and Beyond

- Review the list of virtual field trips that we pulled together to help get you started that is located on our website. We want to grow the list, so please share with us some of your favorite virtual field trips.
- Being purposeful in setting up an on-site field trip will provide a much deeper learning experience for your students. Consider creating a before/during/after exercise:
  - Before: Show a short video to pique curiosity about the event.
  - During: Create a scavenger hunt so students are purposefully looking for specific items.

○ After: Team up students and have them create a presentation for an authentic audience.

> Break away from the confines of the traditional classroom setting. Explore different environments because this can inspire creativity and innovation. New settings help students connect with nature, experience real-world contexts, and incorporate hands-on learning opportunities.

On social media, share your favorite virtual field trip. Tag us and we will add it to our growing spreadsheet for other teachers to use. **#TEACHABLES**

> *Exploration is curiosity put into action.*
> — ATTRIBUTED TO DON WALSH, OCEANOGRAPHER

3.2 With Great Power Comes Great Responsibility: Incorporate Comics and Graphic Novels to Empower Curiosity

As Spider-Man's Uncle Ben once said, "With great power comes great responsibility." As a teacher, you have both of those attributes, and one way to make the most of them is to incorporate comic books and graphic novels into your classroom. The rise in popularity of superhero movies over the past twenty years has given greater visibility to these formats. You have an opportunity to bring these materials into your classroom to help increase the engagement of your students by connecting their interests with content you are teaching. This helps you approach course material from an original angle.

Look at the recommendations below to see how you can get your students engaged and thinking about their learning. And, to quote

Professor X, "The greatest power on Earth is the magnificent power we all of us possess . . . the power of the human brain!"

Recommendations

- Have students write and analyze text to create their own comic book. You can check for application of learning, figurative language, punctuation, content, grammar, and student engagement.
- Use comic book elements as supplementary material for your lesson. For example, you could ask students what makes spider silk such a "super" material.
- Incorporate graphic novels to help students create deeper learning about the content (e.g., studying Martin Luther King Jr. and the civil rights movement, Neil Armstrong and the moon landing). The unique illustrations and vocabulary can increase their interest and help them absorb the content.
- Have students create comic strips that can also be used as formative or summative assessments. They can start with using free comic strip templates from Canva.com or Picklebums.com.
- Students of any grade level can create comic strips to engage with any course content. Here are a few examples of what comic strips can help with:
  - Learning events from history
  - Applying science terms
  - Retelling a story
  - Detailing a timeline of events
  - Sequencing a story or historical events
  - Describing the steps to take when solving a multistep mathematics problem
- Have your students form small groups to research, discuss, and create posters with positive quotes from comic books,

superhero movies, comic strips, and graphic novels. These will be posted on your classroom walls, which is a great way to allow your students to take ownership of their classroom and make it an environment that they enjoy. (See "A Different Look" in section 2.7 for more ideas on changing your room.) Here are some examples to get you started:

- "Why do we fall? So we can learn to pick ourselves back up." (*Batman Begins* movie)
- "Because no matter how small an act of kindness or generosity or simple positivity you put out into the world, it *will* make a difference." (*Wonder Woman* comic)
- "It's your race, and yours alone. Others may run it with you, but no one can run it for you." (*Peanuts* comic strip)
- "Just because someone stumbles and loses their path, doesn't mean they're lost forever." (*X-Men: Days of Future Past* movie)

Above and Beyond

- Storyboard That is a great resource for cooperative groups to use to create a comic strip. The basic features version is free.
- Use Powtoon to create eye-catching animations to teach concepts and lessons. Or better yet, have students partner up to create their own to share with others or as a formative assessment to check for thorough understanding of concepts. There is a subscription cost.
- Have students create comic books using Pixton. You can try it free for seven days and then there is a subscription cost.

Graphic novels and comics spark excitement because of their visual storytelling, which helps with comprehension and attracts different learning styles. They also provide a medium for artistic expression that can make reading more fun.

On social media, share with us how you incorporated recommendations from the "With Great Power Comes Great Responsibility" strategy in your classroom. What did you do and how was it perceived by your students? Please tag us. **#TEACHABLES**

> *Cartooning is hard work sometimes, but at least one has the satisfaction of knowing he has made others laugh.*
>
> — CHARLES SCHULTZ, CARTOONIST

3.3   Mystery Hour: Spark Curiosity with Mystery

"Whoa, I did not see that coming!" How many times have you said that at the end of a movie or book? The next thing that inevitably happens is you want to discuss the twist with someone.

Incorporating mystery and suspense in your classroom is a fabulous way to pique your students' natural curiosity and get them engaged and talking about what's coming next in class. The following recommendations will help your students improve their problem-solving skills, analytical abilities, and communication skills, and these ideas will also unleash curiosity and engagement.

Building a Mystery

Create an escape room filled with puzzles, riddles, and brainteasers that relate to the content you will be teaching. This will take some time and effort, but the results will be worth it. Your students will utilize many skills in an escape room, such as critical thinking, problem-solving, and teamwork. Here are the general steps:

1. Determine approximately how long you want the adventure to last.

2. Decide how many groups of students you will have and how many students per group.

3. Create an engaging story for the escape room or simply tell the students they are taking part in an escape room.

4. Decide what they need to learn and the tasks that need to be completed from start to finish.

5. Have fun creating the escape room tasks. You will need duplicate tasks based on the number of groups you have. Here are some ideas:

   ○ Solve a crossword puzzle, word scramble, word search, or riddle where specific letters are a clue to the next task.

   ○ Practice math skills by solving mathematical problems, assembling geometric shapes, or predicting a pattern.

   ○ Compose a message with invisible ink. To make invisible ink, mix lemon juice with a couple of drops of water in a bowl. Dip a cotton swab into the mixture and write your message on paper. After it dries, hold the paper up to a light to make sure it can be read.

   ○ Find a clue that is hidden in a box, vase, balloon, book, or drawer.

   ○ Assemble a puzzle of a cut-up picture that holds a clue.

   ○ Open combination locks or padlocks.

   ○ Decipher a message in Morse code. (Be sure that students have access to the Morse code language, either in the game or somewhere in the room.)

   ○ Complete an obstacle course. (Students might need to determine how many steps or jumps to take to get from point A to point B correctly.)

6. Make a list of specific help clues you will provide if the students are struggling with a task and ask for a clue.

7. After the students have escaped, have a discussion with them to find out how the game increased their learning of the specific content. Or if you created an escape room as a brain

break, ask them which puzzles they liked the best, which were the hardest, and which were too easy. That way, you have information for the next one.

Recommendations

- Write a question and/or post a picture on the board to pique interest in course content. Tell your students to take the first three to five minutes of class to discuss the question or image with a partner. This will get them asking questions, hypothesizing, and ultimately curious about the learning that will take place.
- Turn the lights down and play a song that will provide a clue about what students will be learning. This will stimulate their interest and get them curious about the lesson. They'll wonder what's going on and you will have hooked them from the start. For example, play "Boogie Woogie Bugle Boy" or "Coming in on a Wing and a Prayer" for World War II lessons, or play "The Butterfly Song" when teaching the stages of the butterfly.
- Display a box with an item inside it to get students at any grade level curious about what they're going to be learning, no matter the content area. Tell students they have five to seven minutes to ask you twenty questions to determine what's in the box. This will improve their questioning techniques, their ability to listen to others, their recall information, and their deductive reasoning.
- Share a mystery with the students through a video or story and listen to their enthusiasm grow as they discuss it.
- Have students investigate a topic they're curious about and present their findings to the class. This is a great idea before the holidays or at the end of the school year when you need to keep everyone engaged and working on their reading, writing,

speaking, and listening skills. For example, students could choose a topic like space exploration and research aspects such as history, unidentified flying objects, or future mission trips.

- Try a Mystery Skype experience. This is a great way to increase student engagement in a lesson, and it also teaches critical thinking, collaboration, cultural awareness, deductive reasoning, digital literacy, geography, and teamwork. Michele Leger has created a newsletter that provides the steps needed to create an amazing Mystery Skype experience with your students. Mystery Skype provides the opportunity for teamwork, collaboration, and friendly competition.

Including mystery in the classroom engages students by tapping into their curiosity and desire for discovery. It creates a sense of intrigue while presenting a puzzling situation or unanswered question. Mysteries prompt students to think creatively, problem-solve, and explore different solutions.

What recommendation did you try from the "Mystery Hour" strategy? Please share a story and/or pictures on social media. Tag and follow us (we follow back) so we can hear how you got your students curious and engaged in their learning. #TEACHABLES

> *Curiosity comes first. Questions can be windows to great instruction, but not the other way around.*
>
> — RAMSEY MUSALLAM, EDUCATOR

3.4 Have You Read This? You Have to Read This!: Promote New Books with Fresh New Titles

According to experts in the white paper by Houghton Mifflin Harcourt, "The major predictor of academic success is the amount of time that a student spends reading. In fact, the top 5 percent of U.S. students read up to 144 times more than the kids in the bottom 5 percent."[8] We all have our favorite books, authors, and genres, and we tend to stay within our enjoyment zone. A great way to encourage students to expand their repertoire is to have a peer suggest a book to them. In your classroom or school hallway, create a space for students to bring in books they would recommend to others. This is a great way to create a community of readers!

Hold a Book Swap

A book swap allows your students to keep their home library fresh and full of new titles. You can organize a book swap in your classroom or perhaps even help coordinate a school-wide event. Because you're trying to get students to expand on what they're currently reading, it's important to encourage them to bring a diverse selection of books to trade with each other. Here are some steps to get you started:

1. Collect books for the swap by asking students to bring one or more in that they are ready to part with. Note: Some students may not have any books to bring in, so check out a local secondhand bookstore to see if they have free books that you can obtain as donations.

2. Create space for displaying the books so that the covers or spines are visible. Try to arrange titles by genre.

---

8   Houghton Mifflin Harcourt, "The Value of Independent Reading: Analysis of Research," *Houghton Mifflin Harcourt*.

3. Be sure to establish swap rules regarding the number of books each student can take.

4. Have each of your students provide a short summary of why they liked the book they brought in and why they recommend it. Note: For a school-wide swap, ask donors to write why they recommend the book on an index card or sticky note.

5. Set a timeline for when students should complete reading their new book. Have them provide the reason they chose the book, explain if it was outside their typical genre, and give a brief summary of the book.

6. There are likely to be books left over that are not going to a new home. You can add these to your classroom library, save them for the next book swap, or donate them.

Recommendations

- To generate excitement about books, schedule a virtual meeting with an author. (See the "Who's the Expert?" strategy in section 3.5 for more details.)

- In language arts classrooms, allow students to give a quick book talk (three to five minutes) when they complete a book. You need to model how to do this so students learn how to discuss a story without giving away too much—just enough exciting details to entice other students to read the book.

- Decorate a shelf to encourage students to look at one another's books. If a student has completed a book and highly recommends it, they can place the book on the shelf and put a sticky note with their name on it. That way, others know to ask that student specific questions about the book. This is a great way to encourage students to talk more about what they're reading.

- Provide dedicated reading time each day. Language arts classrooms need to allow ten minutes of uninterrupted classroom time for students to read a novel of their choice. Of course, there must be tight guidelines in place. It doesn't happen overnight. *The Book Whisperer* by Donalyn Miller offers tips that can create a classroom of readers.

- Once or twice a year, have students write a letter to the author of a book they read that inspired them. You can have younger students collectively craft a letter to the author of a read-aloud picture book. Authors may even write back to your students.

- Create a special place in your classroom for elementary or primary students to read to stuffed animals or dolls. Reading aloud without the pressure of their classmates listening will help students gain confidence and comfort with reading. This is a great way to improve fluency and reading skills.

- Implement reading buddies by pairing a younger student with an older student who will read to them. The younger ones will love that the big kids read to them, and they will create a strong and safe relationship with one another.

- Participate in World Read Aloud Day, created by the non-profit LitWorld and sponsored by Scholastic. This occurs on the first Wednesday of February. On the website you can get a free kit that includes resources, activity sheets, discussion guides, and more.

- Hold a "book tasting" during which students "taste," or sample, a selection of books that you've chosen ahead of time. They can rotate among tables to sample the books and record notes about the ones that interest them. You can also hold a variation on this event in which students place two of their favorite books on their desk and everyone walks around the classroom scanning the various books, taking notes, and making a list of the ones they'd like to read next. This is a great way to get students talking more about the books they're reading.

- Organize a "musical book preview" (think musical chairs) to allow students to review a wide variety of titles. Create a circle of chairs in your classroom, hallway, gymnasium, or another space that can accommodate everyone. Place one book on each chair, play some fun or peaceful music, and have the students begin walking in a circle. When the music stops, students pick up the book that is on the seat they're in front of. They sit, look at the cover, read the synopsis on the back of the book, and/or scan the pictures. When the music begins again, the students stand, put the book down, and resume walking around the circle. Complete the process four or five times depending on the age of your students. This will provide an opportunity for students to review various titles and genres that they might not normally take a second look at. Have students create a list with their top two or three titles that they want to read.

- Create a reading library (containing books, comic books, graphic novels, and/or magazines) in your classroom.
  - Include books that reflect your students (e.g., multicultural, home language, abilities, race, gender).
  - Provide books that are diverse in genre (e.g., poetry, historical fiction, science fiction, mysteries, fantasy, biographies).
  - Provide books for your students' grade level, but also include books below and above their grade level.
  - Review the list of elementary-level books we've compiled. Our selections cover topics such as mental health, autism, and Down syndrome. If you have books for any grade level to suggest, please send us an email so we can add it to the growing list.
- Investigate how to get a book vending machine for your school. Here are a few things to consider:
  - Book vending machines are costly, so talk with your PTO or local businesses to see about getting a grant for the funds needed.

- ○ Once you have the funds, determine when students can get a new book (e.g., for acts of kindness or reading efforts, on birthdays or half birthdays). The goal is that each student will get one new book during the school year.
- ○ You should provide the reading level for the books and decide if students can pick any book or if they should pick one for their reading level.
- ○ Make sure you have a couple of champions at the school who can oversee issues that will inevitably come up (e.g., jammed books, refills needed). Plan for how you will keep this program running. Read "The Benefits of Bringing a Book Vending Machine to Your Schools," an article from Edutopia, for great information to help you start your investigation.
- Have a school-wide day or block of time that focuses on the joy of reading no matter the content area. This will help promote independent reading and instill how important it is to take the time to read. A fun way to change things up is to have teachers switch classrooms to read to other students.
- Organize a book club for your students. This can occur before school, during lunch, or after school. Let each student take a turn picking the book to read for the month.

Above and Beyond

- Who doesn't love free? The National Center on Improving Literacy has a section called Kid Zone! that provides access to free e-books. The age range is from three to ten-plus years old, and students can read, listen, or play games (via app, video, or web) to increase their comprehension, language development, phonemic awareness, phonics, vocabulary, and writing skills. They also provide a Resource Repository for you to find reliable sources that they recommend.

- Share "Reading 101: A Guide for Parents" from the National Education Association with parents and guardians to provide activities they can do at home to help their child with reading. This is for pre-K to second grade but would also help teachers at any grade level who have second-language learners in their classroom.

One of Mrs. Navarrete Maxfield's eleventh-grade students at the Integrated Learning Center is so confident in his writing that after every story he writes he says, "This should be published. They should make it into a movie."

Share how you've incorporated more reading in your class. What changes did you make and how have they affected your classroom environment? Please tag us. **#TEACHABLES**

My most prized possession was my library card from the Oakland Public Library.

— BILL RUSSELL, ATHLETE

3.5 Who's the Expert?: Building on Knowledge from a Skilled Professional

Having a guest expert in your classroom is a wonderful way to provide students with valuable information, a different perspective, and real-world experiences. Experts can hook kids on a new unit of study and extend their understanding beyond the regular curriculum. Using experts can help students see the relevance of their learning in the real world. Inviting an expert to your classroom can also increase students' engagement.

The guest expert can be a parent, guardian, or community member, but truly, the sky's the limit in our virtual world. You can invite people from any profession to provide their expertise to enhance your lesson. If you can think of it, you can find it. Remember your classroom stretches beyond its walls.

When you schedule a guest expert, use the following steps to make their visit a success:

- Provide information to the guest expert such as the grade level, how much time they have to speak, what your students already know (generally), and what you would like the expert to speak about.
- Encourage the guest expert to teach the class rather than just talk at the students. Suggest they make it interactive and/or hands-on.
- Have your students prepare questions and provide them to the guest expert ahead of time.
- Debrief with your students to make the most of the learning.
- After the visit, have your students thank the guest speaker for their time and expertise by mailing individual notes or drawings or by creating and sending a word cloud with text relating to what they learned. (You can use Free Word Cloud Generator or WordClouds.com, among other tools.)

Recommendations

- Ask for help from your community members, local businesses, and parents and guardians. There are experts everywhere. Additionally, the expert can join the classroom more than one time. As students learn more about the expert's topic, they may have more questions that the expert can answer.
- Consider using a virtual platform in your classroom to connect and collaborate with a class from outside your city, state, or country. This is a fabulous way for students to learn from

one another and see classrooms from different cultures. You can also connect with other teachers using a social media platform such as Instagram, Facebook, or X (formerly known as Twitter) to learn more ideas and solicit advice.

- Use a video conferencing tool such as Skype, Zoom, Microsoft Teams, or Google Meet to connect with an expert (e.g., a college coach or athlete, a college professor, an artist, an actor, a screenwriter, a farmer, a hotel manager, a plumber, a construction worker, a chef, or a cosmetologist). This takes you beyond your community and opens up a plethora of opportunities for students to learn.

Above and Beyond

Get your colleagues on board to help you schedule an expert conference for your students. Organize a half-day conference at your school with multiple experts from your community. Each student will get to choose two or three expert sessions to attend. After the conference, the students will need to debrief and discuss what they learned.

> A student in my Integrated Learning Center (ILC) class who fairly recently became wheelchair bound always had the dream of being an artist. She thought she wouldn't be able to do that anymore, so I found an artist who is in a wheelchair to show her that it did not limit her abilities or squash her dreams.
>
> **—TYLER, SEVERE NEEDS SPECIAL EDUCATION TEACHER**

On social media, tell us who your guest expert was and what your students learned. Please tag us. #TEACHABLES

> *In a completely rational society . . . the best of us would aspire to be teachers, and the rest of us would have to settle for something else.*
>
> — LEE IACOCCA, AUTO EXECUTIVE

3.6 Dose of Dopamine: Engagement through Movement

There are times in a school day when engagement is low and the mood just needs a boost. Students often have stressful feelings before beginning a summative or standardized test, so sometimes they need some laugh- ter to put everything into perspective. Laughter creates a positive learning environment, which fosters relationships between students and teachers.

Incorporating dance and fun activities promotes physical movement and helps students release stress, enhancing their overall well-being and focus. By using some of the recommendations below, students of all ages can get a nice dose of dopamine dumped into their brains, turning a sad day into a happier one.

Recommendations

- Dance and sing along to these songs: "Macarena," "Y.M.C.A.," "Chicken Dance," the Charlie Brown song, "Cupid Shuffle," "Cha-Cha Slide," or "Hokey Pokey."
- Use GoNoodle.com to get your students up and moving. There are loads of free videos organized by topic, such as mindfulness and mental health or outdoors and the environment. (See the "Play the Music" strategy in section 3.10.)

- Have students periodically stand and move around. They could touch their toes, stretch their hands high over their head, hop, walk around the room, skip, or jog in place. Ask your students for suggestions.
- Show a funny video clip (three to five minutes) to your class. You could select a clip from *America's Funniest Home Videos*, an appropriate comedian, or another clean, funny, and appropriate source.
- Go to ZooBorns.com to ooh and ah while looking at baby animals from around the world. This is a great opportunity to learn more about animals too.
- Have students share something about themselves with a classmate. It could be their favorite video game, favorite place to visit, someone they consider a hero, or something else.
- See the "Breathe, Enjoy, and Have Fun" bonus strategy in section 5.1 for more recommendations.

Above and Beyond

Tell your students jokes and let them share a few of their favorites (though you may need to approve the jokes first). We've also compiled a list of jokes and riddles for you. Please share your jokes with us so that we can add to this growing list.

> Enjoyable classroom experiences make learning more engaging, creative, and motivational, which leads to improved knowledge retention and academic success.

Please share with us your favorite way to lighten the mood in your classroom. Be sure to tag us on social media! #TEACHABLES

> *New research suggests that dopamine, the chemical which controls pleasure and memory in the brain, can be used to hijack motivation and increase attention spans among learners.*
>
> — AMANDA ROLLINS, AUTHOR

3.7 What Are You Passionate About?: Create Passion Projects

Students have many things they want to learn more about, but not every interest will be covered in your standards. What if, one hour a week, students were given time to research, explore, and create something they are personally interested in? This hour could easily help you to discover a student who loves to draw, code, or organize.

Companies across the globe are implementing time for their employees to create, explore, and learn. Why should we have students wait until they're adults to start thinking about their passions? Let's tap into their inquiring minds and let them start discovering right now.

Recommendations

Passion projects will take a little more time and effort, but once students understand the process, they'll be ready to research! Here are the steps we suggest:

1. Share something you are personally passionate about with your students.
2. Let your students orally share the things they want to learn more about, and then have them jot down their ideas in their interactive notebooks (or take notes for them).

3. Next, carve out sixty minutes during the week for students to begin researching their interests. Some may change their minds about their topics numerous times, and that's OK.

4. Next, look online for examples of students' passion projects and share those with your class.

5. Together as a class, create a rubric that includes all the specifics for presenting the passion projects. You can research online for examples that are targeted to your grade level.

6. Have the students decide on a platform or format to use for presenting their projects to an authentic audience (e.g., PowerPoint, iMovie, Prezi, a skit, or a demonstration).

7. The authentic audience will have the rubric in front of them so they can score the presenter and provide feedback.

8. As an after-action review (AAR), have a class meeting and discuss what went well, what needs to be improved for next time, and whether this was a meaningful project that promoted interest and learning.

9. Wait a couple of weeks and begin the process all over. Students may continue with their original topic, modify it as a result of recommendations received, or research something brand new. Remember to make tweaks based on the AAR.

Above and Beyond

In a world where innovation is the key to solving the smallest and largest of problems, there is nothing more fun than hosting an invention convention. This activity cultivates creativity and critical thinking skills among students as they work in groups to brainstorm and develop innovative solutions to real-world problems. It promotes teamwork and collaboration, and it enhances communication and presentation skills. Students can showcase and explain their inventions to their peers and teachers. The hands-on learning experience allows students to engage in the entire process of invention, from the problem-solving idea or to their final design. The invention convention can be a classroom or school activity or a district-wide event. Read the article titled "How to Hold an Invention Convention in Your School" from Houghton Mifflin Harcourt to get ideas plus downloadable templates to help your students as they create their inventions.

> Passion projects allow students to explore their interests and develop a sense of purpose, fostering intrinsic motivation and deep engagement while they learn. This is a great opportunity for your students who finish an assignment or task early to continue learning and creating.
>
> A good teacher can teach a class. A great teacher can create a future.
>
> Yes, it's a teacher's job to instruct a class of students, However, if the students only remember it as a class, then there is nothing great about it. If they remember the teacher, then they remember the time and effort from them. A great teacher is remembered and recommended. Supporting and understanding their students allows them (the teacher) to be a better step for the students' success. Think of it like a clock made up of several gears. Only the big ones are noticed which likely have a significant role in the system. A great teacher is one of those big gears.
>
> **—MATHIEU, FORMER FIFTH-GRADE STUDENT, NORTH DAKOTA**

Share your students' passion projects on social media. Please share pictures and advice and tag us. **#TEACHABLES**

> *Small successes can add up to major achievements.*
>
> — SHAWN ACHOR, AUTHOR

3.8 Smell It, Feel It, and See It: Spark Excitement

Interactive learning is great for engagement, and it helps students to cement course content by using their senses. The idea of using different types of stimuli is called dual coding, and it helps learners to encode information in their brains more effectively, which allows that information to be more easily retrieved later on.

Students may read about the different battles of the Revolutionary War, watch a short video, and take some notes. But when they actually *create* the battlefields out of clay and teach others about the events, they will better understand and remember the material because of dual coding.

Recommendations

- Use kinesthetic movements to make connections to learning. Examples:
  - When learning about angles, have students jump at a ninety-degree angle or make a ninety-degree angle with their arms.
  - When learning about grammar, have students clasp their hands to represent the conjunctions that bring words together.
  - When learning the word *sway*, have everyone get up and sway like a tree in the wind. (This works for all kinds of words, scientific terms, and more. Students love to act out their learning.)
  - Have students respond to a question by moving to a specific place in the room that is designated as Strongly Agree, Agree, Disagree, or Strongly Disagree.

- Have elementary and primary students take a knee beside their desk to indicate when they have all their school supplies prepared and are ready to learn.

- If students take notes on a video, lecture, or reading, make sure they incorporate images that go with the text. This helps cement the learning through dual coding because it works both sides of the brain. They can draw the images themselves too. For example, when learning about Pearl Harbor, students can draw an image to go with all vocabulary words related to the lesson.

- Have students use clay or Play-Doh. For example, students can create a plant cell and label its parts, create and label the four stages of a butterfly, create angles and geometric shapes, or work on fine motor skills while writing letters into the clay. Secondary students like to use clay and Play-Doh too! This is a great way for you to check for understanding.

- Students can create parodies to help them learn new content or recall important facts and skills. *Schoolhouse Rock!* is a prime example of why this helps learning stick. (See the "Play the Music" strategy in section 3.10 on ways to incorporate music in your classroom.)

Above and Beyond

- The six-minute video "Whole Brain Teaching, High School" showcases amazing movement-based techniques and strategies to include in your classroom. In addition to the great dual-coding technique, notice the pacing, engagement, total recall, hands-on teaching and learning, and so much more. See how the teacher even helps students remember the correct page number.

- "The Powerful Effects of Drawing on Learning" is a video from Edutopia that provides information from a study that found "students who drew information remembered nearly twice as much as students who wrote it." Watch the two-minute video to see why implementing drawing in your classroom will benefit your students.

> Engaging all of a student's senses when teaching will enhance their learning by creating connections and reinforcing memory retention. When you incorporate auditory, visual, kinesthetic, and tactile strategies into instruction, students are more likely to retain new learning, experience a deeper level of engagement, and understand the content much better. Words alone do not convey meaning. Students have to interact with the content in order to move it from short-term to long-term memory.

Please share with us on social media any methods you use to help your students engage their senses while they are learning. And be sure to tag us! **#TEACHABLES**

> *[When I was young,] I not only liked the pictures and the stories [in library books] but the feel and the smell of the books themselves.*
>
> — JUDY BLUME, AUTHOR

3.9 I Wonder: Wonder Walls Engage Curiosity

We need to help students develop their curiosity. When we get deep into learning, students will have random questions or will want to learn more about a specific facet of the content. We need a place to house these additional thoughts and questions because we don't always have time to address them during a regular class period, but we don't want to lose the opportunity for additional learning. When students ask questions, you know they're engaged.

Wonder Walls help develop curiosity and are an excellent extension to learning. They are literal walls, bulletin boards, or poster boards where students post topics they're interested in or have questions about. Wonder Walls provide the space for curiosity, engagement, and deeper thinking to continue even after the lesson is complete.

Remember that students of all ages have questions and want to know more. Keep that curiosity and engagement strong.

Recommendations

- Create a Wonder Wall and encourage students to place sticky notes on it when they think of something they would like to know more about (or a new topic altogether). For example, when discussing diseases, a student might write a note that says, "Where do pandemics begin and how do they spread?" All student questions can increase engagement and deepen learning.

- When concluding a lesson or to cue learning for the next day, talk about a few of the sticky notes on the Wonder Wall. The Wonder Wall is also a great way to start or end the day when you find yourself with an extra three to five minutes.

- Have students talk in small groups about their learning, and encourage them to create a few questions that might intrigue other classmates. Then have them post the questions on the Wonder Wall. This is a great way to deepen content learning. It can also extend the level of learning by incorporating ideas and questions that haven't been covered in the lesson or textbook.

- Have a student or group of students research the answer to an unknown question that is on the Wonder Wall and share it with the class. This is a great opportunity to help students realize that even as a teacher, you don't always have the answer.

Above and Beyond

Padlet is a great tool for creating a digital Wonder Wall for each class period or subject in upper elementary, middle school, and high school classrooms. Students can easily post additional questions pertaining to a specific subject in class using their phone, tablet, or laptop. Using Padlet keeps your classroom walls free for other material. We've created an example for you on our website.

> Providing a Wonder Wall is the perfect addition to your inquiry-based classroom (a learning environment that promotes curiosity and engagement).

Take a picture of your Wonder Wall, post it on social media, and tell all of us how your students responded to and utilized the wall for their learning. Please tag us. **#TEACHABLES**

> *In a place where every learner is encouraged to reach his or her dreams, these "what ifs" can become reality.*
>
> — GEORGE COUROS, EDUCATOR AND AUTHOR

3.10 Play the Music: Songs Increase Engagement

Music is at our fingertips and can be quite powerful; it stirs both our emotions and our senses. It can increase engagement and give students (and you) a short brain break (three to five minutes). Music provides a time to relax and breathe or get up and move. The songs you play can be connected to your content, create structure for transitions, build curiosity, help set the mood, or simply be enjoyed.

Lyric Lesson

This interactive and engaging lesson is designed to enhance and develop your students' critical thinking, figurative language, grammar, reading fluency, summarizing, and communication skills. Each daily lesson, lasting approximately six to eight minutes, spans five days. Each day focuses on different aspects of the chosen song and its associated lesson plan. The goal is to encourage critical thinking by inferring the intentions of the song's author. For example, why did the author write the song? What do you think the author's mood was when they wrote the song? You can have students choose a song that they love to listen to or have them find a song that relates to a specific topic you are teaching. This activity is great for the start of the class period or day.

STEP 1: Develop a lesson plan for students to follow when sharing their song, or utilize the lesson plan we provided on our website.

STEP 2: Prior to assigning the activity, model the lesson and the template to ensure students understand the process.

STEP 3: Approximately two weeks prior to a student's presentation, they must submit their selected song, along with the lesson plan and lyrics for you to review.

STEP 4: Once approved, the student will create a PowerPoint with the lyrics and highlight specific elements like vocabulary, inferences, and figurative language that coincide with the lesson.

STEP 5: Student presentation.
1. Day one (approximately eight minutes):
   a. The student will present the PowerPoint and teach the lesson based on the plan.
   b. Play the song for their classmates to follow along with the lyrics.

    c. The class will discuss inferences, vocabulary, and the type of figurative language being used in the song.

    d. You will provide feedback to the student based on criteria such as creativity of the PowerPoint, eye contact, voice, and high-level questioning.

2. Day two (approximately six minutes):

    a. The student will ask their classmates if they have any questions that need to be clarified and if they changed their inference after having time to think about the lyrics from the previous day's lesson.

    b. Play the song for the students to continue practicing their reading fluency while singing along with the lyrics from the PowerPoint.

3. Day three (approximately six minutes):

    a. Play the current week's song.

    b. Randomly choose a student to pick a previous song. You or a student will play the song and PowerPoint for the class. (See the "Everyone? Everyone?" strategy in section 2.8 for ways to randomly choose the students.)

4. Day four (approximately six minutes):

    a. The same as day three.

5. Day five (approximately six minutes):

    a. Select two random students and let them each select their favorite song from previous lessons. You or a student will play the song for students to continue practicing their skills and having fun.

Use AZLyrics.com to get accurate lyrics to songs. Here are examples of songs that have a deep meaning and work well with this lesson:

    a. Tim McGraw's "Humble and Kind"

b. Blackpink's "Don't Know What to Do"

c. Sam Cooke's "A Change Is Gonna Come"

d. Ugly Kid Joe's "Cats in the Cradle"

e. Daniel Powter's "Bad Day"

f. Katy Perry's "Firework"

g. Lionel Richie's "Hello"

Prepare to be impressed by the significant boost in reading fluency achieved through this enjoyable process. Your students will have the chance to explore a variety of music genres shared by their classmates. The lyric lesson could easily become the highlight of your day and your students' day. It's simple to create a class playlist, weaving in the songs taught by your students. As the school year draws to a close, you'll find yourself with a memorable collection of your students' most beloved tunes.

Recommendations

- Create classroom playlists that you can use for calming time, transitions, and get-up-and-dance times.

- Ask students what their walk-up song is and play a portion of it as they walk to the front of the classroom for presentations, demonstrations, or class teaching. Be sure to keep track so that you play each student's walk-up song at least one time during the school year. (See the "Getting to Know You" strategy found in section 1.3.)

- Play an instrumental song and have students close their eyes and take deep breaths in and out before they take an exam or conduct a presentation. Or they can do it just to center themselves.

- Play music that connects to your content. For example, play songs from the 1920s when studying the Roaring Twenties, play songs from contemporaries of Leonardo da Vinci when discussing his art and inventions, or blast "Playing with the

Boys" by Kenny Loggins prior to teaching volleyball in PE class.

- Find songs to help students remember content, such as songs naming US presidents, discussing the Bill of Rights, or listing the fifty states in alphabetical order. There are also songs about measurement, the periodic table, and the solar system.
- Show *Schoolhouse Rock!* videos to enhance learning.

Firework

When coaching, I often model specific lessons for teachers so they can see them in action. After I modeled a personification lesson using Katy Perry's "Firework" song, I received these letters from two fourth-grade students.

Dear Mrs. Abla,

Thank you for making class time positive this morning. It made me get excited for class today. You helped me learn the meaning of personification. Now if I become a writer I know how to make a good book. You helped me know how to hook my reader to my paper. You made me feel good about myself and my work. Now if I write a good paper I won't let anyone tell me otherwise. You would make a great teacher. You are a firework that can be seen across the world but mostly at J. Elementary School. So, thank you Mrs. Abla! You helped me have confidence in my writing. You could be an international teacher.

—**ASHLEY**

Dear Mrs. Abla,

Thanks for showing me to never give up and taught me to shine and be the best person. I honestly didn't know a song could teach you so much. Thanks for coming all this way just to see us. Thank you for teaching us so much just for showing up at our school. I personally think your the best teacher ever. Don't tell anyone. J. Elementary is so happy and I will make the school a better place. I think your the best firework and a really good teacher and keep on shining bright making other schools be the best we can be. Don't forget your making the world a better place. You made us very happy. Thank you.

—YOUR FRIEND, GEORGE

Regularly revisit your goals and reflect on your progress. Assess the impact of the changes you've made and make any necessary adjustments along the way. Remember, reflection is an ongoing process that helps us grow as professional educators.

Tell us on social media how you have incorporated music into your classroom and how it has affected your classroom environment. Please tag us. **#TEACHABLES**

> *Bach takes you to a very quiet place within yourself, to the inner core, a place where you are calm and at peace.*
>
> — YO-YO MA, MUSICIAN

Story: Hurling in the Pentagon

One of the greatest things about being an educator is getting to take students on field trips to provide a deeper level of learning. It heightens engagement and increases curiosity about the content. I encourage educators to move the learning beyond the classroom as often and as much as possible.

Teaching is the best profession because students are unpredictable. The excitement lies in never knowing what might happen when you're halfway across the country with them. I can officially say I had a student hurl in the Pentagon. Probably the first and only one ever! I had my group of fifth graders on a tour of the Pentagon and I looked over at Trent. He was looking a little pale. When I approached him, he said he thought he might vomit. I asked the very strict military guard if we could please have a trash can to carry with us in case he got sick. The guard kindly told me that was against their protocol. We were also not allowed to go into the bathroom unsupervised, so we carried on. I was really starting to worry, so I then asked the guard at the back of our small group if we could get Trent to a bathroom. Once again, he nicely said not on this tour because it would take him away from his post. The Pentagon has beautifully spotless tiled floors everywhere, so I thought it would be an easy cleanup if the worst-case scenario should happen.

We proceeded into the 9/11 memorial chapel when I heard it! This was the only place in the Pentagon where there was beautiful royal blue carpet. Here is the funniest part of the whole event: those two military guards who were in control of every move we made had no idea what to do at this point. They were deer in the headlights with looks of pure panic on their faces! They called for backup, the backup arrived, and still no one knew where to begin. I asked if we could please get Trent to the bathroom before it happened again, and one of the guards escorted us to the bathroom. I was able to get another parent to stay with my group of students while I got Trent cleaned up. The guards hurried my group of students out of the memorial chapel and closed it to other groups. With a big grin on his face, Trent proudly stated, "I threw up in the Pentagon!" We joked about the fact that he will be telling this story when he's a grandpa someday.

Curiosity is the engine of achievement.

— SIR KEN ROBINSON, EDUCATOR AND AUTHOR

Chapter 4

High Expectations

WE'VE ALL SEEN THAT TEACHER AND CLASSROOM. You know. The one where the students are confident, focused, and happy. The one where the teacher gives specific directions and the students immediately know what is expected and follow the requests. The one where those same students score high on benchmarks and standardized tests.

Do you want to know one of the ingredients for this success? It's simple: the teacher has set high expectations for the students and genuinely believes that every single student can learn, grow, and succeed. The teacher believes in and encourages the students, and in turn, the students believe in themselves too.

Deep down, students must believe that their teacher knows they can learn. If students are certain the teacher sees their potential, and they receive encouragement, acknowledgment of effort, and positive feedback, then they will work hard to meet their goals. Not only do students feel confident when a teacher sets high expectations, but the teacher is also more effective—which affects *their* attitude toward teaching.

However, the opposite also holds true: "If the teacher doesn't believe I'm smart," a student might reason, "then I must not be." It is imperative that you support each student and help them climb the ladder to success. We're going to say it again: teachers must set high expectations and truly believe that *all* students can learn.

Every teacher wants to look out into the classroom and see students who are eager to learn. A key to being *that* teacher is to build strong and trusting relationships (as we discussed in chapter 1) but also to help students set specific and relevant stretch goals. These goals will have a strong effect on students' achievement and commitment to their learning. But those goals need to be talked about and revisited often to stay meaningful.

The strategies in this chapter will provide specific ideas that you can implement to construct an encouraging and high-achieving classroom. When you see the potential in every student, and you combine that vision with strong teaching practices, you will make a huge impact on student learning.

Above and Beyond

Watch the compelling five-minute video "Carol Dweck—A Study on Praise and Mindsets" and you will quickly understand the power of your praise and the effect it can have on your students' learning.

> *People in a growth mindset don't just seek challenge, they thrive on it. The bigger the challenge, the more they stretch.*
>
> — DR. CAROL DWECK, PSYCHOLOGIST

High-Expectations Activity

Stop here and take a few minutes to reflect on how you go about setting high expectations for your students. Think about how you work with them to accomplish their goals. Answer the following yes-or-no statements. If you answer no to any of them, use the space below to make notes on how you can change that no to a yes.

1. I have procedures in place that students manage themselves.

2. I pause during lessons to check for understanding.

3. The homework I give is relevant to the students' learning.

4. I use images, graphic organizers, and kinesthetic activities to support the learning.

5. I provide rubrics.

6. I use sentence stems to deepen the learning.

7. I communicate learning intentions and success criteria.

8. I encourage students to wonder and ask questions.

9. I link achievement to motivation, effort, and goal setting.

10. I manage behavior positively and proactively.

11. I set specific goals with students that are regularly reviewed.

12. I allow for student voice.

13. I transfer the responsibility of the learning to my students.

14. I work with all students equally.

15. I support and encourage risk-taking.

16. I monitor the time I spend talking versus the time students are talking and collaborating.

17. I have things planned and in place so my students are actively learning bell-to-bell.

18. I chunk learning so that students are successful, and I check for understanding throughout the segments.

19. I ask thought-provoking questions.

20. I make sure students are applying their learning.

21. I have projects in place that enrich the learning and go beyond basic recall.

> *If you think you can, you can. And if you think you can't, you're right.*
>
> — MARY KAY ASH, ENTREPRENEUR

4.1 The Power of Effort: Working Hard = Success

As Carol Dweck puts it, "We like to think of our champions and idols as superheroes who were born different from us. We don't like to think of them as relatively ordinary people who made themselves extraordinary."[9]

We are all extraordinary in our own ways, and it's important that students understand the correlation between effort and achievement. In life there will be struggles, and how a person responds to those challenges is completely up to them. We need to instill in students that rarely is one successful without perseverance, grit, and determination.

Recommendations

- Remember to share your own struggles—and the skills that helped you to persevere. When you reveal your challenges, you help your students see you as real, understanding, and approachable.
- Have students place a number (from one to five) at the top of their paper to indicate how much effort they believe they put into an assignment or quiz. After the assignment is scored, provide time for students to reflect on their effort and how it correlates with their score. Reinforce trust and honesty.
- Provide examples of people your students might be able to relate to who have overcome challenges. Professional athletes and famous people are not the only ones who have faced difficulties, so try to find people within your community.
- Invite guest speakers (either in person or via video) to talk about struggles they overcame. See the "Who's the Expert" strategy located in section 3.5 for steps to take so your students get the most out of the experience.

9 Carol S. Dweck, *Mindset: The New Psychology of Success* (New York: Ballantine Books, 2007), 90.

- Compliment students when they expend effort and show grit. This goes back to the "Caught Ya" strategy in section 1.2, but it also reinforces student effort and the importance of a growth mindset.
- Share specific videos and stories of people expending effort. Sports have great examples, but also try to include other areas where children and adults have had to work hard to achieve something. Share your own stories and have students share theirs if they choose to. Here are some examples:
  - J. K. Rowling's *Harry Potter* was rejected by twelve publishing companies. In a 2016 tweet, the author wrote, "I wasn't going to give up until every single publisher turned me down, but I often feared that would happen." We are glad that she didn't give up on her dream.
  - Author Jack Canfield stated, "*Chicken Soup for the Soul* was rejected by 144 publishers. If we had given up after 100 publishers, I likely would not be where I am now." Encourage students to reject rejection. If someone says no, just say "Next!"
  - Oprah Winfrey overcame a challenging upbringing and other obstacles to become one of the most influential media personalities in the world. Despite experiencing poverty, abuse, and racial discrimination, she persevered and worked her way up from local radio to hosting her own talk show and establishing her own media empire.

Above and Beyond

- Enjoy a three-minute CBS newscast on the power of hard work and determination. Steve Hartman talks about his journey from school janitor to principal.

- US Olympian Wilma Rudolph had polio as a child but still managed to be an Olympic gold medalist. Watch a three-minute video about her.
- Driving with no arms takes some extra effort. An eight-minute video of Richie Parker shows you just how amazing this feat is. Trust us, you want to watch this one.
- Using the word *yet* can transform your classroom. If a student says "I can't get it," help them learn to rephrase this message in their head: "I can't get it, yet." You can share the two videos below to introduce the word *yet* into students' vocabulary:
  - Hip-hop artist C. J. Luckey's four-minute music video of his song "The Power of Yet" has catchy lyrics and is great for primary and elementary students. It's a perfect launching point for teaching students about a growth mindset.
  - *Sesame Street* teamed up with Janelle Monáe for a cute two-minute song called "Power of Yet." Primary students may want to get up out of their seats to sing and dance along.

There's something magical that happens when students make the connection between their own lives and what you teach. That's when you know you have made a difference.

Dear Mrs. Abla,

I would like to thank you for helping me get my grades from bad to good! When I was struggling in reading you helped to get my grades up and now I'm back on track to succeed.

The other reason I was not doing so well is I was not trying as hard as I could have but you motivated me to work hard and get a great education. I also learned

> how to work hard to get into a good college and get a great education.
>
> **—IZZY, SIXTH GRADER, COLORADO**

On social media, please provide a specific example of how you promote effort in your classroom. Be sure to tag us! **#TEACHABLES**

> *Provide an uncommon experience for your students and they will reward you with an uncommon effort and attitude.*
>
> **DAVE BURGESS, EDUCATOR AND AUTHOR**

4.2 Do You Get It?: Check for Understanding

During a lesson, it's important to review learning targets, check for understanding, and determine who may need extra support. A fast and easy way to gather this information is to simply ask.

In a safe environment, students will feel comfortable asking questions. In those contexts, asking for help should be seen as a positive because it demonstrates that students want to learn. There are numerous ways to check for understanding and encourage students to ask for help, and they can all provide you with valuable information.

Recommendations

- Check for understanding by asking a question and having students give a thumbs-up or thumbs-down response. Alternatively, students can use a three-finger rating: one finger means they don't understand, two fingers means they understand a little, and three fingers means they understand.

This allows them to quickly show their perceived comprehension. It's a great opportunity to reinforce the importance of a growth mindset, and it shows students that it's fine to sometimes fail. It's important to help students understand that we "fail forward" when learning or trying something new.

- Provide items (cups, laminated paper) that are red, yellow, and green. Students can use these to nonverbally indicate their level of understanding: red means they need help, yellow means they have questions, and green means they're good to go.

- While the rest of the class is working independently or collaborating, meet individually with students who need additional support.

- Try implementing Ask Three, Then Ask Me. When a student has a question, they must first ask three of their classmates for help before asking you. Enforce this recommendation by asking "Did you ask three before me?" when a student asks you a question. If they say no, then reiterate that they need to ask three classmates first. If they have consulted their peers, then help them, of course. When the class is knee deep in an activity, creating something, or simply using technology to complete a task, having specific question processes in place can help eliminate frustrations and tempers—especially if you're short on helpers.

- Have students summarize their learning by drawing a picture, writing a tweet in 280 characters or less, or recording a one-minute video.

- Use an entry ticket system at the beginning of your lesson to find out what students recall from the previous day or what they might know about an upcoming topic. Review students' responses while they complete bell work or do-now work. (See the "Let's Get This Learning Started" strategy located in section 2.2 for ideas.)

- Use an online assessment that checks for understanding, gives you immediate feedback, and is fun for your students (e.g., Kahoot!, Quizlet, Nearpod, Formative).
- Ask "What questions do you have?" instead of "Does anyone have a question?" That way, your students know you want to take the time to make sure they completely understand the content.

Above and Beyond

There is a link on our website to a comprehensive list of valuable online resources that will help you assess how well your students are understanding the concepts you're teaching. Common Sense Education provides a list of online formative assessment tools that provide quick and easy ways to check for understanding.

> Ask students what they think the purpose of school is. This can help you enhance their understanding of the importance and privilege of being educated. Students will tell you if you simply ask.
>
> The purpose of school is to educate students because they are the future of the world. They need to learn how to solve problems and learn about problems that occurred in the past, so they know how to not make the same mistakes. Students also need to learn how to make a life for themselves that they are happy in.
>
> —CASSIDY, ELEVENTH GRADER, TENNESSEE

What recommendations have you used in your classroom from the "Do You Get It?" strategy? Post your response on social media, tag us, and follow us (we follow back). #TEACHABLES

> *On your worst day, you are someone's best hope.*
>
> — UNKNOWN

> *Lors de votre pire jour, vous êtes le meilleur espoir de quelqu'un.*
>
> — INCONNUE

(We have included this quote in French [from Google Translate] to model the recommendation from the "Where in the World?" strategy in section 1.7, where we advise you to use multilingual quotes in your classroom.)

4.3 One Size Doesn't Fit All: Differentiate Homework

Do you know why you're giving homework? Are you differentiating the homework? Does the homework enhance your students' learning? Keep in mind that as Nancy Paulu stated, "Homework is meant to be a positive experience and to encourage children to learn."[10]

Think about homework as practice that extends learning and doesn't just justify a classroom grade. A homework assignment must be relevant and meaningful, and it must help students grow in their learning. The worst form of homework is the kind that's assigned just because "that's what we do" or "that's what the parents and guardians expect." When you give homework, be sure to review it and provide specific feedback to the students, otherwise they'll wonder why they needed to complete it. (See the "Dollops of Feedback" strategy in section 4.6 for tips on providing good feedback.)

---

10 Nancy Palau, *Helping Your Students with Homework: A Guide for Teachers*, US Department of Education. https://eric.ed.gov/?id=ED416037.

Recommendations

- Differentiate homework for your students so all are learning and succeeding without frustration. In the classroom we differentiate our teaching based on students' learning levels, language acquisition, level of family support, physical needs, or whatever the case may be. If you differentiate in the classroom, please make sure you differentiate the schoolwork outside the classroom as well.

- Homework should take a minimum amount of evening time to complete independently. Remember that your class may not be the only one your students have homework for.

- When assigning a project to be completed at home, contact parents and guardians to ensure that all students have the materials needed to complete the project. If they don't, be prepared to send materials home with students, or you can modify the project. Always ask yourself if the students' work and effort will be worthwhile.

- Use homework to frontload and build curiosity around the next day's new learning. Have your students read a short article, watch a short video, watch a commercial, ask a guardian a question, or do something that will help build excitement and interest. This creates relevance and homework buy-in as well.

- Explain to your students the significance of the homework assignment so they understand the purpose and benefits of their effort.

- Whenever possible, have the homework be applicable to everyday life so students see the relevance of their learning.

- Provide information to parents and guardians to make sure they have a clear understanding of what their role is in the homework process.

Above and Beyond

Watch Edutopia's one-minute video "Homework: How Much Is Too Much?" and reflect on your beliefs about the purpose of homework. If an assignment is worth students' time, it should be relevant and you should provide feedback.

> This Integrated Learning Center student clearly articulates the importance of a strong relationship with their teacher, Mrs. Navarrete Maxfield, who can easily calm them so they can succeed regardless of how hard a math assignment might be.
>
> > I ask [for] help with math and they calm me down when I get scared. They calm me down with math.
>
> **—TENTH-GRADE ILC STUDENT, COLORADO**

What homework policies do you have in your classroom and school? Please share on social media and be sure to tag us. **#TEACHABLES**

> *Homework is a complicated thing.*
>
> — DR. LYN CORNO, EDUCATOR

4.4   Working Walls: Resources for Everyone

Unlike traditional wall displays, Working Walls are interactive. Their purpose is to support students in their current learning and enable them to grow and become more independent. Working Walls are a resource providing information students need to help them learn the content. There can be sentence stems or resources like pamphlets, notes, and images that the students can refer to or remove and take to their desks.

A Working Wall is the second educator in the classroom. It grows, changes, and evolves over the semester or school year. It reflects your students' needs, what they're learning, the relevance of the content, and specifics of where they need support.

Recommendations

- Use sentence stems for questioning, discussion, or writing in different content areas.
    - What surprised me was . . .
    - I think that . . . because . . .
    - First . . . then . . .
    - In my opinion . . . in addition . . .
    - I agree with . . . because . . .

- Use images and vocabulary that are up to date with what you're learning in the classroom.
- Provide web addresses with additional material to aid in the learning.
- Visit the wall often with your students to remind them of its great resources.
- List students' expertise on the wall so classmates know who they can go to for additional help or guidance. Post each student's name followed by their specific strength (e.g., PowerPoint, Excel, Word, editing, creativity, music, coding, encouragement, computation).
- Hide little clues on the wall and see how quickly the students find them. This will let you know how often the wall is being used.

Above and Beyond

If you'd like to see some examples of how to use a Working Wall, take a few minutes and research them on Pinterest or Google. You'll find all different types for all different grade levels.

Working Walls are a great way to encourage your students to be independent learners.

Take a picture of your Working Wall, post it on social media, and tell us how this has impacted the learning in your classroom. Tag us, please. **#TEACHABLES**

> *Never be limited by other people's limited imaginations.*
>
> — DR. MAE JEMISON, ASTRONAUT

4.5 Unpack, Engage, Teach, Process, and Check: Planning for Learning

All effective and challenging lessons have five key components: unpack the standard, create a hook for engagement, direct teach, process through academic talk, and check for understanding. Below are a few must-haves for you to be intentional with every lesson and to engage all students in the learning.

We need to remember that our purpose is not to disseminate information in hopes that students will learn what wonderful information we are sharing; it is to ensure that *all* our students are grasping and retaining the content we are teaching.

Recommendations

- Establish a hook that makes all students want to learn more. Make it exciting! (See the "Let's Get This Learning Started" strategy in section 2.2 for ideas.)
- Create a student-friendly learning target. Post it and discuss it with your students to check for understanding. Be sure to

refer to it often throughout the lesson to help your students make the connection between their learning and the target.

- As often as possible, include images, graphic organizers, opportunities to create, and movement in your teaching and learning. This will activate both sides of your students' brains to engage and cement learning. The more you involve students, the more they will retain the new learning.

- Check in to make sure all your students understand the main points of your lessons. This can be done as you go through a lesson or at the end. This check-in doesn't have to be extensive, but it does need to be completed. Examples include exit tickets, randomly asking students questions to check for understanding, online quizzes, writing two sentences about the most important takeaways from the day's lesson, or writing a newspaper headline or tweet.

- Have your *why* answer ready when students ask questions like "Why do I need to know this?" and "When will I use this as an adult?" We've provided a few answers for you:
  - History provides us with ways to learn about ourselves and how we came to be, and it also helps us avoid mistakes and create better paths for our society.
  - Art gives us many different outlets to express our creativity and our feelings.
  - Science can lead to technological advances, and it can help us learn about enormously important and useful topics, such as our health and the environment.

Above and Beyond

- Students must process information to own it, so here are a few techniques from the Interaction in an Instant tool in *Tools for Classroom Instruction That Works*,[11] which Cheryl coauthored.

---

11   Silver et al., *Tools*, 75–79.

(See the "Is It Really Cooperative?" strategy in section 2.9 for additional techniques.)

- ◦ Give One, Get One: Provide students with a question and tell them how many total responses you want them to collect. Have the students think of two or three responses on their own. Next, they need to find a partner and share *one* of their responses and get *one* response. They will continue this until they get the total number of responses you indicated. Finally, they need to share or summarize the information they collected.

- ◦ Mix-Pair-Share: Have students stand up and then ask them a question that they need to think about. When you say "mix," the students walk around the room until you say "pair." Students will share their response to your question with the student closest to them.

- Make cross-discipline connections for your students. Here are some examples:

  - ◦ Have students write a persuasive letter to a manufacturer or particular company they've been learning about during their environmental studies.

  - ◦ The very best way for students to learn content is to teach others. Have students use their writing, collaboration, cooperation, and creating skills to create a quiz or game board that other students can play while practicing their new skills in a fun way.

When a teacher has high expectations and creates strong, positive relationships with their students, the outcome can be limitless. It's easy to tell when a teacher is a warm demander because they push their students while being there to support them along the way. This is a nice example of just that:

My favorite teacher was my science teacher I had my sophomore year, the class was biology. He was everyone's least favorite because of how hard the class was but I really liked the challenging dynamics of it. Sometimes we wouldn't even talk about the lesson but just talk about our opinions on different topics like how the universe was created. He actually listened to what we had to say and helped us all have an open mind. He would always say it's okay if we're not completely understanding the entire process of cell division or what not as long as we tried to learn something. His goal was to make us actually think about stuff. He also said a lot of things that stuck with me like "The truth doesn't change whether you believe it or not."

—HANNAH, ELEVENTH GRADER, OKLAHOMA

Please snap a picture of your students engaged in a lesson where you've used an "Unpack, Engage, Teach, Process, and Check" strategy. Post it on social media, tag us, and follow us (we follow back). **#TEACHABLES**

A well-designed hook should capture students' interest, get students thinking about the relevant content, and help students activate prior knowledge.

HARVEY F. SILVER, CHERYL ABLA, ABIGAIL L. BOUTZ, AND MATTHEW J. PERINI, EDUCATORS AND AUTHORS

4.6 Dollops of Feedback: Offering Specific Feedback for Improvement

Have you ever given so much feedback to a student that they walk away with their paper in hand wondering, "Where do I even begin to make this better?" That's oversaturation.

Providing specific and corrective feedback on what the student did well and telling them what the next steps are will help to improve their learning. By putting on your coach's cap and giving feedback that is specific, you provide that "just-right" dollop of feedback.

Recommendations

- Teach students that the best way to give feedback is by using the Oreo technique: provide a positive compliment (cookie), provide an area that could use improvement (filling), and seal it with another positive (cookie).
- Provide students with a *glow* (positive feedback on what is correct or well done) and a *grow* (what needs to be improved). Teach your students how to provide glows and grows to their peers.
- Cover students' names when assessing an assignment so that you're not making assumptions about their work.
- Make sure that feedback is tied to the learning target. Reference the target when you're providing feedback so that your students make the connection.
- Use criterion-referenced feedback (rubrics). You must provide the rubric prior to an assignment because students need to know exactly how their work will be assessed. Take a little time to go through the rubric and, if you can, show an exemplary project as an example.

- Conference with students to provide specific feedback on their efforts (e.g., "It's clear that you've been practicing because your welds are becoming smoother").

- Give quick and nonspecific nonverbal feedback for encouragement (e.g., thumbs-up, high five, smile, nod).

- Use statements or questions that begin with "I noticed . . ." or "Have you thought about . . .?"

- Use Google Docs or Microsoft Word whenever possible so you can track changes and add comments to provide thorough feedback.

- Periodically ask students to provide you with feedback on your teaching and tell them why you are requesting it from them. Provide a specific question or two for them to answer so it will be more useful to you as you learn and grow. Be sure to thank your students for the feedback and let them know within a few days how you will be adjusting things based on what you learned from them. Here are some example questions to ask:
    - How did today's activity help you learn?
    - How can I more clearly explain the rules of the game?
    - What was your favorite part of this lesson and why?

- Put stickers or stamps on students' papers. Students, no matter what age, love seeing these on their papers. Watch the TED talk in the "Above and Beyond" section for proof.

Teaching Self-Assessment

Create rubrics with your students so that they can increase their understanding and take ownership of their learning. Students tend to set the bar much higher when they contribute to the process.

Engage students in a brainstorming session to generate a list of criteria for the rubric.

1. Critically look at the criteria list and categorize similar ideas together. Discuss and refine the criteria as a group.
2. Collaboratively establish different levels of performance for each criterion. Using a scale of one to three is most beneficial and simple for students. You can also use a smiley face, neutral face, or sad face emoji with primary students.
3. Review the rubric as a whole, make necessary adjustments, finalize it, and distribute it to students for use during the assignment.

Remember, these steps can be adjusted and customized based on the specific needs and preferences of your classroom and students.

Above and Beyond
Watch Professor Nick Fuhrman's "The One Thing All Great Teachers Do" TED talk. It's twenty-three minutes long, but we promise you'll laugh. He talks about how great teachers celebrate mistakes, appreciate differences, relay feedback, and evaluate themselves. He tells a story about the one time he didn't put encouraging stamps on his college students' papers and one specific student's reaction. You have to watch to hear the full story.

You never know the impact your words, your body language, or a simple note might have on the life of your students. Remember to make the extra effort.

I love writing short personal notes to my students about an act of kindness I witnessed or how proud I am of them for accomplishing a specific task. One specific boy in my ILC class would always coyly come up at the end of every class period and ask if he would be getting a note that day. His mom told me that he keeps all the notes that I write to him even though he can't read them on his own. One short note can make a difference.

—TYLER, SEVERE NEEDS SPECIAL EDUCATION TEACHER

On social media, share how you provide specific and corrective feedback to your students to help their learning. Please tag us. **#TEACHABLES**

> *Research shows that less teaching plus more feedback is the key to achieving greater learning.*
>
> — GRANT WIGGINS, EDUCATOR

4.7 Quest to Discover: Ask Higher-Level Questions

Asking higher-level questions helps to engage your students in a deeper level of thinking and learning, and all students have the right to go on this knowledge quest. Tough inquiries also encourage students to think beyond the literal and move on to the analysis, synthesis, and evaluation phases of thinking. However, it takes time, work, and practice to generate higher orders of questioning.

Recommendations

- Be prepared for higher-level questions by coming up with simple sentence stems. Here are some examples to get you started:
  - "When did _____?" "How would you describe _____?" (This aids memory.)

- ◦ "What is the main idea of _____?" "Which is the best answer _____?" (This aids understanding.)
- ◦ "What examples can you find to _____?" "What would the result be if _____?" (This aids application.)
- ◦ "What do you think of _____?" "What ideas justify _____?" (This aids analysis.)
- ◦ "What would happen if _____?" "How would you test _____?" (This aids evaluation.)
- ◦ "How could you determine _____?" "Why was it better than _____?" (This aids creation.)

- Students love to sound like mathematicians during a math class, scientists during biology, and writers during language arts, so why not provide them with the tools to do just that? Give your students a list of excellent sentence-starter questions and let them practice using them in small groups. You can model what this would sound like first. Here are some examples of sentence stems for you to share with your students (you can modify them as needed):
  - ◦ Mathematician:
    - ▪ "To solve this equation, we can apply the principles of . . ."
    - ▪ "By employing mathematical modeling techniques, we can gain insights into . . ."
    - ▪ "The proof for this theorem relies on the fundamental principle of . . ."

  - ◦ Scientist:
    - ▪ "Based on the experimental data, we can conclude that . . ."
    - ▪ "Through statistical analysis, we identified a significant correlation between . . ."
    - ▪ "The results of our study suggest a potential mechanism for . . ."

- Writer:
  - "The opening paragraph of this piece sets the tone by . . ."
  - "By employing a metaphor, the writer highlights the underlying theme of . . ."
  - "The author's choice of words creates a powerful emotional impact, evoking . . ."
- Historian:
  - "The historical context of this event can be understood by examining . . ."
  - "By analyzing the social, economic, and political factors of the time, we can better comprehend . . ."
  - "The historical significance of this event lies in its impact on . . ."

- We want students to do more than simply read words. When an article or a section of a textbook might be a little harder for them to understand, you can use reciprocal teaching to get students to think more deeply about the text and increase their comprehension. Put your students in groups of four and assign each student one of the following specific roles:
  - Summarizer: Summarizes the written material
  - Predictor: Predicts what is about to take place in the passage
  - Clarifier: Clarifies vocabulary and words that are a little challenging
  - Questioner: Creates questions from the text and questions that make you think beyond the text

- Have students write higher-level questions based on the content you teach. Use the following schema to explain the difference between lower-level and higher-level questions:

- Lower-level questions are easily located in the text or lecture. Here are examples:
  - Who are the characters in the story "The Three Little Pigs?"
  - What types of materials did the pigs use to build their houses?
- Higher-level questions are the ones that incorporate feelings, creativity, and connections. Here are examples:
  - What would have happened if the first little pig had built his house out of adobe?
  - How would you feel if you were the wolf and all three pigs were in the brick house?
  - What is an alternative ending you might write for the story?
- Prepare higher-level questions prior to your lessons and post a cheat sheet for yourself.
- Prepare rigorous questions for your second-language learners who are still developing their language acquisition skills.
  - Have them draw, point to an image, or provide sentence stems to communicate their understanding of the concepts.
  - Use the Record and Transcribe features on a computer.
  - Play Four Corners by assigning the corners in the classroom as A, B, C, and D. Ask multiple-choice questions and have a student go to the corner that best represents their answer. Students who are learning English as their second language may not be able to read all the choices or say the answer, but they can certainly show they know the content by going to the correct corner.

Above and Beyond

- Read Cheryl's Edutopia article "How to Ask Questions That Engage Young Students" for additional tips on how to make learning more joyful for your students.
- San Bernardino City Unified School District created the eight-minute "Using Reciprocal Teaching to Engage 3rd Grade Readers" video. This is an example of a teacher using reciprocal teaching in the classroom. You can use the process in classrooms from elementary through high school. You can use any type of material that you're having your students read for understanding (e.g., articles, textbooks, novels, comic books).

> The best type of teacher is one who asks their students how they learn best and then creates a classroom that fits that type of learner. Hands-on learning, group projects, supportive, and believing in their students is the best!
>
> **—ADDIE JO, ELEVENTH GRADER, OKLAHOMA**

Please share with us on social media what you tried and how it worked for you and your students. Please tag us! **#TEACHABLES**

> *Teacher-initiated questions enhance student learning by developing crucial thinking skills, reinforcing student understanding, correcting student misunderstanding, providing feedback for students, and enlivening class discussion.*
>
> CHRIS A. CARAM AND PATSY B. DAVIS, AUTHORS

4.8 Failing Forward: Failing Is How We Learn

Do your students understand the expression "failing forward"? It captures the same idea as the growth mindset, which according to Carol Dweck is the "belief that your basic qualities are things you can cultivate through your efforts."[12] Failing forward is just a catchier version that students tend to understand a little better.

We want to build a growth mindset in students so that they understand the power of trying something, failing in the attempt, learning from the attempt, and trying it again or differently to get the desired results. You know the old saying "When the going gets tough, the tough get going"? Don't give up! Try, try, again!

Recommendations

- Support and encourage risk and inquiry within your classroom. Praise and model risk-taking and reinforce that it is brave to ask questions and to admit you don't know and need/want help. (See the "Do You Get It?" strategy in section 4.2.)
- Celebrate failing forward in the classroom when students try new things that may not be perfect the first time. Celebrate the trying.
- Have students teach a lesson on what it means to grow through failure. They can create a PowerPoint, lecture, or short quiz and craft strong questions to help their fellow classmates think deeper about what it means to grow or learn through failure.
- Share stories of when you yourself have failed at something. This honesty will help students by showing that not everything came easy to you and that you were not always successful.
- Create a failure board in your classroom. Every time someone tries something new and doesn't succeed, have them place that task on the board and celebrate the effort they put into it.

---

12 Dweck, *Mindset*, 7.

Make sure to discuss the individual failures with the student and determine next steps they can take.

Above and Beyond

- Share videos and stories about learning from failure that your students can relate to. Here are a few short ones that may be appropriate to share with your students:
  - Angela Duckworth says effort counts twice. Watch her six-minute "Why Effort Matters More Than Talent" video to find out why.
  - John Legend talks about "success through effort" and says that "every successful person has failed at what they love to do." Watch a two-minute video from Khan Academy to hear more.

- Watch "Grit: The Power of Passion and Perseverance," a six-minute TED talk by Angela Duckworth about her theory on grit and success.
- Watch the thirteen-minute TED talk called "Resilience: The Art of Failing Forward." In her talk, Dr. Sasha Shillcutt explores the power of vulnerability in embracing professional and personal failures, which leads to increased resilience. By sharing our mistakes, seeking perspectives, and letting go of self-shame, we cultivate a growth mindset.

A school in Texas has a copy of every teacher's diploma posted outside their classroom door. Underneath the diploma is a list of all the areas the teacher has struggled in or failed at. This is to help students understand that failing is all part of the growing and learning process.

Take a picture of your failure board, post it on social media, and tell us what impact it has made in your classroom. Be sure to tag us. **#TEACHABLES**

> *Only those who dare to fail greatly, can ever achieve greatly.*
>
> — ROBERT F. KENNEDY, POLITICIAN

4.9 Students as Teachers: Provide Students an Opportunity to Teach

As teachers we see that when students engage with one another in the teaching and learning process, they retain content better. In fact, research from *Memory & Cognition* found that "students who believe that they will have to teach material to others remember more information than students who are told that their learning will be measured by a test."[13] It's one thing to ask students how they like to be taught; it's another to let the students teach one another or the whole class the way they like to be taught.

So, why do we still see teachers at the front of the classroom doing all the talking, reading, or questioning? As educators we need to learn to release the power and provide students opportunities to teach small groups or the whole class. Sure, it takes some upfront work, but isn't our goal to improve the thinking and learning of all students? As a bonus, students will learn what it feels like to instantly succeed when teaching another student. It becomes a win-win.

---

13 Rhonda Rosenberg, "Benefits of Students Teaching Students," United Federation of Teachers (September 3, 2014): 1–2.

Recommendations

- Release the power! Here are steps to get you started:
  1. Create a lesson plan template that students can use to teach any lesson with few modifications. Show them an example lesson as a guide.
  2. Model the process with the class and then model it again. They should completely understand the expectations of being the teacher.
  3. Remind students that the lesson they will be teaching to the class or small group should be engaging and comprehensible for everyone.
  4. Let students know that if a formative assessment reveals that not everyone understands the content, they will need to reteach to the students who need review or enhancement.
  5. Remember to celebrate the process and the effort it took for students to teach the content. It may not be pretty the first or even second time, but as they practice, they will improve.
  6. Encourage students to create or perform to increase engagement. They can use skits or props, for example.
  7. Just like you, students can incorporate clay or Play-Doh into their lesson to increase engagement and to check for understanding.

This engaging process might take a little time to initially create, but it is always well worth the effort! This strategy works for pre-K through twelfth grade, and all students can be active participants. Students can partner up or work in groups of three, promoting collaboration and enhancing the variety of the lesson they create.

Above and Beyond

- Record yourself teaching a lesson. Watch the recording, and every thirty seconds, note who is doing the talking. This will provide you with data that shows whether you need to incorporate more opportunities for students to talk about their learning to one another.
- Have a colleague or administrator visit your classroom and gather data on who's doing the talking. During a regular lesson, have the colleague set their silent timer and make a note every minute of who is talking. Together, look at the data and see who's doing the most talking. Remember we want as close to fifty-fifty as possible.

The benefits of having your students teach a lesson are plentiful. They will conduct research, practice their presentation and speaking skills, and enhance their knowledge as they take ownership of their learning.

On social media, tell us how it went when you had your students do the teaching. Provide the pros and cons so we can all learn from your experience. Please follow and tag us. **#TEACHABLES**

> *The person doing the talking is doing the learning.*
>
> — UNKNOWN

Story: Allison, a Beautiful Butterfly

Students walk into your classroom with history. You may know pieces of it or nothing at all, but either way, setting high learning expectations for and with each student will show that you believe they can and will succeed, no matter their circumstances. Helping them along their path and seeing the potential they have can help them see themselves as being successful. You may never know where they land once they leave your classroom, but perhaps one day you'll get a friend request. It is incredibly amazing how the belief a teacher has in their students is oftentimes played out in how students begin to see themselves.

I was blessed to teach this precious little girl, Allison, in fourth, fifth, and sixth grade. She had the misfortune of losing her mother in third grade, and she came to my classroom extremely shy and quiet. I could tell instantly that this young lady had an incredible mind. She would read continuously, rarely raising her hand to respond or answer questions, but one-on-one she was a very deep and intuitive thinker. I quickly realized I should not praise her or draw attention to her in class, as that embarrassed her. But I wanted her to share more so that all my students could enjoy the depth of her thinking. I knew I had to be crafty to get her to talk, share her thought process, and find her voice. She slowly began to emerge out of her cocoon like a beautiful butterfly.

Since the class had been together throughout fourth grade, Allison entered fifth grade with close-knit friends who enjoyed her quirky habits and behavior. When you spend that much time together, you begin to find the precious gifts and strengths each person brings to the classroom family. Allison began to share her gift of writing. She created engaging lessons to share with the classroom, shared her outside-the-box thinking, and loved going on field trips, especially to Washington, DC. In fact, she got lost in the United States Capitol building because she was reading every caption, looking at each portrait, and taking in every bit of knowledge. It didn't take long for security to call me. This was day two of our trip, so I made certain that from then on Allison was always in my group as we toured the many other locations.

When the end of sixth grade arrived, I reflected on this special class I had the privilege of teaching for three years. They had all grown into amazing young adults, but the greatest transformation was Allison. Originally quiet and meek, with long dark hair to cover her face, she had transformed into this beautiful, vocal, creative, and delightful friend and classmate.

Last year, Allison reached out to me on Facebook (she said she made an account only to get in touch with me) and asked if I could meet her for dinner. She was a sophomore at a university and was excelling. As I sat there waiting for her to arrive, I wondered what this twenty-year-old might look and be like. In walks this delightful young woman, head held high, dressed in lovely vintage clothing that I quickly learned she had purchased from a secondhand store. It was embellished and added to her beautiful creative flair. We had a lovely dinner catching up on life, other classmates, heartbreaks, and funny memories from grade school, but what I remember the most is her simply mentioning my belief in her, how I'd said she could be and do anything she set her mind to. Believing that all students can learn and grow—and acting on that belief—can make all the difference in a student's life.

> *There are no shortcuts to life; hard work is the only way to go. Strive to be the best you can be and remember that when you try your best, you can't ask any more from yourself and people can't ask any more from you.*
>
> — MICHAEL CHANG, ATHLETE

Chapter 5

Bonus Strategies

AS YOU ALREADY KNOW, OR ARE QUICKLY LEARNING, TEACHING CAN BE ONE OF THE MOST DIFFICULT AND JOYFUL PROFESSIONS, ALL WITHIN A SINGLE CLASS PERIOD. As you teach, you have a great deal of responsibility. You're doing your best to help students learn, grow, and be prepared for their futures. So, we have created two bonus strategies to assist you in your classroom and your life outside of school.

The first bonus strategy, "Breathe, Enjoy, and Have Fun," is all about providing fun brain breaks for you and your students. You know those times when you look out at students' faces and realize you should pause? This strategy provides a number of recommendations, such as playing a game, conducting a scavenger hunt, or having a celebration.

We created "Self-Care" specifically for you because teachers are a dedicated group of professionals who too often forget that they need to stop and take care of themselves. To enjoy your vocation, you must take the time to focus on yourself and your happiness. We see you and we want you to know that you are important, appreciated, and valued, so please take some time to replenish your bucket of joy and energy.

> *When someone doesn't keep an element of play in their life, their core being will not be light. Play gives us the irony to deal with paradox, ambiguity and fatalism.*
>
> — DR. STUART L. BROWN AND CHRISTOPHER C. VAUGHAN, AUTHORS

5.1 Breathe, Enjoy, and Have Fun: Make Memories

This is a bonus strategy for those times when you simply want to enjoy yourself and let your students be kids. There are specific times of the school year that are ideal for taking a breather and enjoying one another, such as the first couple of weeks of school (as your students are learning the procedures and processes), right before an extended break, and the last week of school. Or it might be time to take a fun break after a high-stakes test, during indoor recess, in the middle of a particularly tough week, or simply when you see the need on your students' faces.

As hard as you try to make your precious time with students serious and academic, it's easy to become frustrated with their lack of effort or retention. So, instead of letting learning become stressful, think about fostering social and emotional well-being for all of you. It's important for students to understand that it's all right to take a breath and have fun. The following strategies are simply about enjoying the moment. Be sure to join in on the fun!

Setting Out on a Scavenger Hunt

Keep some prepared scavenger hunts in your back pocket for when your class needs a brain break. You will provide written clues for your students to find something or mini problems for them to solve. The hunt can simply involve activating the mind and body by moving around, collaborating, problem-solving, and laughing. Or it could be tied to the content you're teaching, which is a bonus. The hunts don't need to be elaborate, just fun!

Here's how to get started:

1. Design a clue sheet and make sure you have all the objects that students will need to find.
2. Place the objects around your classroom, school, or outside if you take the hunt outdoors.
3. Divide the students into pairs or small groups of no more than four. You want to keep the number low so that all the students can take part in the hunt.
4. Depending on the grade level, you can either give the groups all the clues at one time (upper grades) or provide one clue at a time (younger students).
5. Review all the solutions to make sure each group has solved the clues correctly.
6. Discuss the hunt and the outcomes. Even if it wasn't tied to a specific lesson, learning still took place. Ask your students, "What worked well? What are lessons learned for next time? Did everyone contribute to the solutions? What did you learn?"
    - There are many different types of scavenger hunts that you can create. Here are some examples:
        - Pictures: they need to find specific pictures around the room that are the answers to the clues.
        - Revision: provide a key topic and the students must find four specific pieces of supporting material.
        - Shapes: provide specific shapes such as a hexagon, cube, pyramid, and oval. The students must find these shapes and identify them.
        - Geography: provide descriptions or features and have students identify which city, state, or country it is.

Recommendations

- Bring in your favorite board or card game and have the students play it. Not only is it fun to take a break, but games are great for working on social skills, collaboration, communication, and good sportsmanship.
- Provide choices for students to get creative (e.g., paint, clay, Lego blocks, shaving cream, Minecraft, magnets, crayons).
- Find one fun day to celebrate each month in your classroom—or better yet, get the whole school involved. You can provide a few options and let your students vote. The NationalDayCalendar.com and NationalToday.com websites have thorough lists of special and unique days and months to celebrate. Note: one of our favorites is National High Five Day (third Thursday of April). Who doesn't like to get and receive a high five?
- Create game boards/bingo cards (e.g., with vocabulary words, mathematics answers, sight words, or state capitals) for your students to play with. They will have so much fun while also learning. Use BingoBaker.com to create your own cards or search for a ready-made card.
- Play a Jeopardy game using ready-made templates on JeopardyLabs.com. You can also build your own. The students will enjoy the friendly competition while learning!
- Create a Connect 4 board by drawing six circles across and down on the whiteboard. Split your class into two teams and then ask a question. Have each team write their answer on a sticky note (you will need two different colors) and put it in one of the circles. Check the answers. Students with correct answers get to keep their sticky note in the circle chosen, while the incorrect sticky note gets removed. Have the teams play until one of the teams gets four in a row.

- Go classic and play games such as Simon Says, Hangman, twenty questions, or charades. The game can connect to learning while getting your students to move and have fun.
- Start the school year off by providing a list of items that your students need to find in the classroom or in the school. When everyone has completed the scavenger hunt, have a celebration.

Building relationships with students, demonstrating genuine care, and sharing a sense of joy can impact their well-being on any given day.

Jesus, a kindergartener in the school where I volunteered for AmeriCorps in Austin, Texas, snuck out of his class one day in order to give me a love note that contained hearts. On the day of his kindergarten graduation, none of his family members were able to attend so he spent the whole day with me. He was such a sweet boy and I tried my best to make the day special for him.

—TYLER, AMERICORPS LITERACY FIRST TUTOR

On social media, share a "Breathe, Enjoy, and Have Fun" strategy you implemented with your class. Please tag us! We are so excited to hear what you did and how it went. **#TEACHABLES**

Children shouldn't be overly scheduled. They should have blocks of time to promote spontaneity and creativity.

— DANIEL LEVITIN, AUTHOR AND PROFESSOR

5.2   Self-Care: Activities to Focus on YOU

Practicing self-care is one of the most important things you can do for yourself. It involves taking care of your psychological, emotional, spiritual, personal, professional, and physical health so that you can be your best. We've provided recommendations to help get you started, and we encourage you to commit time each day to self-care and to finding what brings you relaxation and joy.

You can also share and implement these recommendations with your students so that they can learn the importance of self-care.

Recommendations

- Make it a habit to take a minimum of fifteen minutes every single day for self-care.
- Breathe. It may sound easy because we're constantly doing it, but take time to stop and purposefully take slow, deep breaths in and out.
- Give someone a long and heartfelt hug.
- Look in the mirror and finish an "I am" statement with positive affirmations (e.g., "I am funny," "I am intelligent," "I am hardworking," "I am positive," or "I am kind").
- Get up and get your blood flowing. Enjoy a walk outside, walk or skip up and down your stairs, stretch, or dance.
- Find something that brings you joy and makes you smile or laugh. It could be a specific photo, video, movie, or memory.
- Give someone a sincere compliment.
- Go outside and enjoy the beauty of our planet. Look around and observe the butterflies, flowers, trees, people, buildings, or sky. Breathe in the air as you listen to the breeze, birds, traffic, or silence.
- Play your favorite songs and dance until you're out of breath.
- Cuddle up with a loved one, which could be a human or pet.

- Put away all electronic devices for a specific amount of time and do something you enjoy like reading, exercising, cooking, watching a movie, knitting, or napping.
- Write a note/letter to someone to say hi, to thank them, to share that you're thinking of them, or to say that you'd like to get together. Be sure to mail it—because we think it's safe to say that anyone would get excited to see an actual note/letter in their mailbox.
- Be kind to yourself. Say only positive things about yourself like you would to a friend or loved one.
- Take a mental health day and fully enjoy it guilt-free!
- Write in a gratitude journal each night before going to sleep. Include three positive experiences from the day and/or what you are grateful for in your life.
- Journal about how you're feeling on a daily or weekly basis.
- Find an organization that you are passionate about and volunteer.

Above and Beyond

Watch author and happiness expert Shawn Achor's twelve-minute "The Happy Secret to Better Work" TED Talk. It's amusing and informative.

> As we noted earlier in the book, we recommend that you keep those sweet notes, pictures, and pieces of positive feedback in a special place so when you're having a tough day or just need an "I am awesome" pick-me-up, you can reflect on all the good work you've done. A few years ago, we had the good fortune of being able to present a workshop to a group of tremendous K–12 teachers on the beautiful island of Guam. This is one of the notes we saved:

> Cheryl and Lisa, your enthusiasm for learning is contagious! You provided so many great tech tools and hands-on activities and I can't wait to apply them in my classroom. You both rock!
>
> **—BENJAMIN, HIGH SCHOOL TEACHER, GUAM**

Share some of your favorite self-care recommendations on social media and tag us. **#TEACHABLES**

> *Always strive to be a better you.*
> — PETE HALL, EDUCATOR AND AUTHOR

> *Salawasna narékahan pikeun janten anjeun anu langkung saé.*
> — PETE HALL, PENDIDIK JEUNG PANGARANG

(We have included this quote in Sundanese [from Google Translate] to model the recommendation from the "Where in the World?" strategy in section 1.7, where we advise you to use multilingual quotes in your classroom.)

Story: Tribute to a Teacher

We began in chapter 1 by asking, "Have you ever thought of what your former students might say about you at your retirement party?" We decided to close out the chapters and strategies with a heartfelt tribute that was written to a teacher who passed away. We were given permission to share these beautiful and deeply personal words. They were written by a former student whose teacher made a tremendous difference in her life over forty years ago. To make this even more special, the student followed in the teacher's footsteps and has been making a difference in students' lives herself for over twenty-seven years.

How do you write a tribute to someone who saved and changed your life forever?

As an 11 year old, I was a miserably unhappy girl who just couldn't understand why I didn't fit in. I thought I was a freak and didn't fully know how I was going to survive middle school. Literally one day I met a teacher who explained to me that there wasn't anything wrong with me, and that I was special, loved, and had so much to offer the world. She nurtured me, taught me how to use a journal as a place to dream, work out frustrations, and make observations about the world around me and how I could use it to help me understand my world. She showed me how to harness my potential, overcome disappointments, and use my curiosity as a force for change rather than a way to annoy my teachers. She saw me cry and understood how hard it was to live in my skin. She protected me as much as she could from bullies, pushed me to focus on the positives in my life, and taught me coping skills I use every single day.

She showed me that I didn't need to fit in when I was born to stand out.

She inspired me to become a teacher who loves first and teaches second.

She made a difference in many lives, but made THE difference in mine.

I'm here and who I am in many ways because she showed me who and what I could be.

I love you, Mrs. Bachus. Please hug my daddy and my brother for me, and enjoy your crown of many stars. You earned them. I will see you again some day.

And thank you. For everything.

—JUSTINE ROGERS, MISSOURI

Book Club Discussion Guide

WE TOLD YOU THAT YOU DIDN'T HAVE TO READ THIS BOOK COVER TO COVER IN ORDER TO START IMPLEMENTING STRATEGIES IN YOUR CLASSROOM. However, our best hope is that you couldn't put this down and began highlighting, dog-earing pages, and making notes as you got more and more excited about how you can make changes in your classroom.

Now that you're nearly at the end, we want you to think about how you're going to follow through and keep your excitement alive. We said that teaching doesn't need to be lonely. Neither does reading this book. Connect with your colleagues to have a book club discussion. We've provided questions for you and would love to hear your responses.

Book Club Discussion Guide

1. Which of the four categories resonated the most with you and why?
    a. Relationships
    b. Organization and Procedures
    c. Curiosity and Engagement
    d. High Expectations

2. Which strategy are you going to implement during your next school day?
3. What story affected you the most?
4. What are three things you can incorporate consistently in your classroom to create a learning environment where everyone belongs?
5. What is the one thing you're going to do for self-care every day?
6. What is a strategy you would include in this book because it had such a profound impact on your classroom environment?
7. If you could ask the authors anything, what would it be? Don't be shy—send us an email and ask.
8. How did this book impact you?
9. How do you think the strategies you're going to implement will affect your students?
10. How did reading this book encourage you to incorporate new ideas to improve the environment for you and your students?

Provide at least one answer to a book study question on social media and tag us. We would love to hear your thoughts and reactions. **#TEACHABLES**

Final Thoughts

AS YOU REFLECT UPON THE STRATEGIES, RECOMMENDATIONS, "ABOVE AND BEYOND" SECTIONS, AND STORIES IN THIS BOOK, REMEMBER TO CAPITALIZE ON THE POWER OF A POSITIVE CLASS-ROOM ENVIRONMENT. And keep this in mind: you are never alone. There are millions of educators worldwide who are working to improve their relationships with students, provide an organized class-room with smooth procedures, purposefully engage their students, and keep expectations high. We come together in schools, through blogs, via videos, and on Instagram, TikTok, Facebook, and X (formerly known as Twitter). There is always another educator who is willing to lend a helping hand.

Being an educator is truly one of the hardest careers, but it's also one of the most rewarding when the pieces come together.

Remember, there is no *I* in teacher, so . . .

- Don't go it alone.
- Encourage one another.
- Offer support and guidance.
- Work with your teammates.
- Welcome student voice.
- Be empowered.

We look forward to hearing from you as you share some of your new strategies from *Teachables* on social media. We celebrate your journey as you travel onward and upward, making a positive difference in the lives of students.

Thank you,
Cheryl and Lisa

> Please share your thoughts about our book on Amazon and social media. Tag and follow us (we follow back) and be sure to use **#TEACHABLES**

Cheryl
- 𝕏 @cherylabla
- 🔗 linkedin.com/in/cherylabla
- ✉ TeachablesBook@gmail.com
- 🌐 sites.google.com/view/teachablesbook/home

Lisa
- 𝕏 @leemaxfield29
- 🔗 linkedin.com/in/maxfieldlisa
- ✉ TeachablesBook@gmail.com
- 🌐 sites.google.com/view/teachablesbook/home

Teachables
- 𝕏 #teachables
- 📷 @Teachables_Book
- ♪ @Teachables_Book
- 📘 Teachables
- ✉ TeachablesBook@gmail.com
- 🌐 sites.google.com/view/teachablesbook/home

> *There was never a time in my youth, no matter how dark and discouraging the days might be, when one resolve did not continually remain with me, and that was a determination to secure an education at any cost.*
>
> — BOOKER T. WASHINGTON, EDUCATOR AND AUTHOR

References

Brewster, Cori, and Jennifer Fager. "Increasing Student Engagement and Motivation: From Time-on-Task to Homework." *Northwest Regional Educational Laboratory* (October 2000).

Dweck, Carol S. *Mindset: The New Psychology of Success*. New York: Ballantine Books, 2007.

García, Lily Eskelsen, and Otha Thornton. "The Enduring Importance of Parental Involvement." *National Education Association* (November 18, 2014).

Hammond, Zaretta L. *Culturally Responsive Teaching and the Brain: Promoting Authentic Engagement and Rigor among Culturally and Linguistically Diverse Students*. Thousand Oaks, CA: Corwin, 2014.

Hamre, Bridget K., and Robert C. Pianta. "Can Instructional and Emotional Support in the First-Grade Classroom Make a Difference for Children at Risk of School Failure?" *Child Development* 76, no. 5 (September 2005): 949–967.

Houghton Mifflin Harcourt. "The Value of Independent Reading: Analysis of Research." *Houghton Mifflin Harcourt*.

Marsh, Helena. "Relationships for Learning: Using Pupil Voice to Define Teacher-Pupil Relationships That Enhance Pupil Engagement." *Management in Education* 26, no. 3 (July 2012): 162.

Palau, Nancy. *Helping Your Students with Homework: A Guide for Teachers*. US Department of Education. February 1998. https://eric.ed.gov/?id=ED416037

Rosenberg, Rhonda. "Benefits of Students Teaching Students." United Federation of Teachers. September 3, 2014: 1–2. https://www.uft.org/news/teaching/research-shows/benefits-students-teaching-students.

Silver, Harvey F., Cheryl Abla, Abigail L. Boutz, and Matthew J. Perini. *Tools for Classroom Instruction That Works: Ready-to-Use Techniques for Increasing Student Achievement*. Franklin Lakes, NJ: Thoughtful Education Press, 2018.

US Department of Education, Office of Safe and Healthy Students. *Quick Guide on Making School Climate Improvements*. National Center on Safe Supportive Learning Environments (2016). Washington, DC.

Acknowledgments

Educators: Thank you for choosing the profession that teaches all the other professions. Your enthusiasm and dedication truly make a difference in the lives of students every day.

Thank you to the amazing Dave Burgess Consulting, Inc., team. You all played an integral part in our passion to bring this book to fruition.

Dave Burgess: You saw our vision and how this book will help EMPOWER teachers.

Tara Martin: Your positivity is contagious!

To the marvelous team at The Reading List, thank you so much for all the behind-the-scenes work you did to help us produce the best book we could create.

Lindsey Alexander: Your patience with our many questions was very much appreciated!

Kaelin Alexander: Your thoughtful ideas and skillful edits were awesome!

Laura Major: Your attention to detail is wonderful, and we appreciate your ability to keep our voice with your edits.

To my awesome friend and coauthor, Cheryl:

This has been an amazing ride and I'm so happy we took it together. Your enthusiasm, expertise, and experience never cease to amaze me. Thank you from the bottom of my heart!

—Lisa

To my dear friend and coauthor, Lisa:

Thank you for always encouraging me to do more, to be more, and to think outside the box. Your attention to detail and beautiful structure have helped this book come to life. Thank you for not giving up on our purpose to help create a more joyful classroom for teachers and students.

—Cheryl

About the Authors

CHERYL ABLA believes sincerely in all students' capacity to achieve at high levels and is passionate about helping educators use their full potential to make a positive impact on students. Cheryl coaches K–12 teachers and school leaders on effective instructional strategies, problem-based learning, classroom technology, teacher coaching, second-language learners support, and creating engaging school cultures and climates. She taught grades 1–12 for over twenty-five years and was the director of two district programs: Parents as Teachers and Migrant Education Even Start. Drawing on her extensive and diverse classroom experience, she has presented at educational conferences around the United States and the Pacific and is a coauthor of *Tools for Classroom Instruction That Works*. Cheryl can be reached at TeachablesBook@gmail.com and on X, formerly known as Twitter, at @cherylabla.

LISA MAXFIELD has worked for educational organizations for over thirty years and currently is a partner success manager and project manager. She assists educators in using observational software, manages projects, conducts technical training sessions, and specializes in building and sustaining lasting relationships with educators, clients, and partners. She enjoys working with educators and is enthusiastic and passionate about helping teachers. Lisa has presented at both Association of Educational Service Agencies (AESA) and Association for Supervision and Curriculum Development (ASCD) conferences and has authored blog posts. Lisa can be reached at TeachablesBook@gmail.com and on X, formerly known as Twitter, at @leemaxfield29.

More from

DAVE BURGESS Consulting, Inc.

Since 2012, DBCI has published books that inspire and equip educators to be their best. For more information on our titles or to purchase bulk orders for your school, district, or book study, visit DaveBurgessConsulting.com/DBCIbooks.

More from the *Like a PIRATE*™ Series

Teach Like a PIRATE by Dave Burgess
eXPlore Like a PIRATE by Michael Matera
Learn Like a PIRATE by Paul Solarz
Plan Like a PIRATE by Dawn M. Harris
Play Like a PIRATE by Quinn Rollins
Run Like a PIRATE by Adam Welcome
Tech Like a PIRATE by Matt Miller

Lead Like a PIRATE™ Series

Lead Like a PIRATE by Shelley Burgess and Beth Houf
Balance Like a PIRATE by Jessica Cabeen, Jessica Johnson, and Sarah Johnson
Lead beyond Your Title by Nili Bartley
Lead with Appreciation by Amber Teamann and Melinda Miller
Lead with Collaboration by Allyson Apsey and Jessica Gomez
Lead with Culture by Jay Billy
Lead with Instructional Rounds by Vicki Wilson
Lead with Literacy by Mandy Ellis
She Leads by Dr. Rachael George and Majalise W. Tolan

Leadership & School Culture

Beyond the Surface of Restorative Practices by Marisol Rerucha
Change the Narrative by Henry J. Turner and Kathy Lopes
Choosing to See by Pamela Seda and Kyndall Brown

Culturize by Jimmy Casas

Discipline Win by Andy Jacks

Educate Me! by Dr. Shree Walker with Micheal D. Ison

Escaping the School Leader's Dunk Tank by Rebecca Coda and Rick Jetter

Fight Song by Kim Bearden

From Teacher to Leader by Starr Sackstein

If the Dance Floor Is Empty, Change the Song by Joe Clark

The Innovator's Mindset by George Couros

It's OK to Say "They" by Christy Whittlesey

Kids Deserve It! by Todd Nesloney and Adam Welcome

Leading the Whole Teacher by Allyson Apsey

Let Them Speak by Rebecca Coda and Rick Jetter

The Limitless School by Abe Hege and Adam Dovico

Live Your Excellence by Jimmy Casas

Next-Level Teaching by Jonathan Alsheimer

The Pepper Effect by Sean Gaillard

Principaled by Kate Barker, Kourtney Ferrua, and Rachael George

The Principled Principal by Jeffrey Zoul and Anthony McConnell

Relentless by Hamish Brewer

The Secret Solution by Todd Whitaker, Sam Miller, and Ryan Donlan

Start. Right. Now. by Todd Whitaker, Jeffrey Zoul, and Jimmy Casas

Stop. Right. Now. by Jimmy Casas and Jeffrey Zoul

Teachers Deserve It by Rae Hughart and Adam Welcome

Teach Your Class Off by CJ Reynolds

They Call Me "Mr. De" by Frank DeAngelis

Thrive through the Five by Jill M. Siler

Unmapped Potential by Julie Hasson and Missy Lennard

When Kids Lead by Todd Nesloney and Adam Dovico

Word Shift by Joy Kirr

Your School Rocks by Ryan McLane and Eric Lowe

Technology & Tools

50 Things to Go Further with Google Classroom by Alice Keeler and Libbi Miller

50 Things You Can Do with Google Classroom by Alice Keeler and Libbi Miller

140 Twitter Tips for Educators by Brad Currie, Billy Krakower, and
   Scott Rocco
Block Breaker by Brian Aspinall
Building Blocks for Tiny Techies by Jamila "Mia" Leonard
Code Breaker by Brian Aspinall
The Complete EdTech Coach by Katherine Goyette and Adam Juarez
Control Alt Achieve by Eric Curts
The Esports Education Playbook by Chris Aviles, Steve Isaacs,
   Christine Lion-Bailey, and Jesse Lubinsky
Google Apps for Littles by Christine Pinto and Alice Keeler
Master the Media by Julie Smith
Raising Digital Leaders by Jennifer Casa-Todd
Reality Bytes by Christine Lion-Bailey, Jesse Lubinsky, and
   Micah Shippee, PhD
Sail the 7 Cs with Microsoft Education by Becky Keene and
   Kathi Kersznowski
Shake Up Learning by Kasey Bell
Social LEADia by Jennifer Casa-Todd
Stepping Up to Google Classroom by Alice Keeler and
   Kimberly Mattina
Teaching Math with Google Apps by Alice Keeler and
   Diana Herrington
Teachingland by Amanda Fox and Mary Ellen Weeks
Teaching with Google Jamboard by Alice Keeler and
   Kimberly Mattina

Teaching Methods & Materials
All 4s and 5s by Andrew Sharos
Boredom Busters by Katie Powell
The Classroom Chef by John Stevens and Matt Vaudrey
The Collaborative Classroom by Trevor Muir
Copyrighteous by Diana Gill
CREATE by Bethany J. Petty
Deploying EduProtocols by Kim Voge, with Jon Corippo and
   Marlena Hebern
Ditch That Homework by Matt Miller and Alice Keeler
Ditch That Textbook by Matt Miller

Don't Ditch That Tech by Matt Miller, Nate Ridgway, and
    Angelia Ridgway
EDrenaline Rush by John Meehan
Educated by Design by Michael Cohen, The Tech Rabbi
The EduProtocol Field Guide by Marlena Hebern and Jon Corippo
The EduProtocol Field Guide: Book 2 by Marlena Hebern and
    Jon Corippo
The EduProtocol Field Guide: Math Edition by Lisa Nowakowski and
    Jeremiah Ruesch
The EduProtocol Field Guide: Social Studies Edition by Dr. Scott M.
    Petri and Adam Moler
Empowered to Choose: A Practical Guide to Personalized Learning
    by Andrew Easton
Expedition Science by Becky Schnekser
Frustration Busters by Katie Powell
Fully Engaged by Michael Matera and John Meehan
Game On? Brain On! by Lindsay Portnoy, PhD
Guided Math AMPED by Reagan Tunstall
Happy & Resilient by Roni Habib
Innovating Play by Jessica LaBar-Twomy and Christine Pinto
Instructional Coaching Connection by Nathan Lang-Raad
Instant Relevance by Denis Sheeran
Keeping the Wonder by Jenna Copper, Ashley Bible, Abby Gross, and
    Staci Lamb
LAUNCH by John Spencer and A.J. Juliani
Learning in the Zone by Dr. Sonny Magana
Lights, Cameras, TEACH! by Kevin J. Butler
Make Learning MAGICAL by Tisha Richmond
Pass the Baton by Kathryn Finch and Theresa Hoover
Project-Based Learning Anywhere by Lori Elliott
Pure Genius by Don Wettrick
The Revolution by Darren Ellwein and Derek McCoy
The Science Box by Kim Adsit and Adam Peterson
Shift This! by Joy Kirr
Skyrocket Your Teacher Coaching by Michael Cary Sonbert
Spark Learning by Ramsey Musallam
Sparks in the Dark by Travis Crowder and Todd Nesloney
Table Talk Math by John Stevens

Unpack Your Impact by Naomi O'Brien and LaNesha Tabb
The Wild Card by Hope and Wade King
Writefully Empowered by Jacob Chastain
The Writing on the Classroom Wall by Steve Wyborney
You Are Poetry by Mike Johnston
You'll Never Guess What I'm Thinking About by Naomi O'Brien
You'll Never Guess What I'm Saying by Naomi O'Brien

Inspiration, Professional Growth & Personal Development

Be REAL by Tara Martin
Be the One for Kids by Ryan Sheehy
The Coach ADVenture by Amy Illingworth
Creatively Productive by Lisa Johnson
Educational Eye Exam by Alicia Ray
The EduNinja Mindset by Jennifer Burdis
Empower Our Girls by Lynmara Colón and Adam Welcome
Finding Lifelines by Andrew Grieve and Andrew Sharos
The Four O'Clock Faculty by Rich Czyz
How Much Water Do We Have? by Pete and Kris Nunweiler
PheMOMenal Teacher by Annick Rauch
P Is for Pirate by Dave and Shelley Burgess
A Passion for Kindness by Tamara Letter
The Path to Serendipity by Allyson Apsey
Recipes for Resilience by Robert A. Martinez
Rogue Leader by Rich Czyz
Sanctuaries by Dan Tricarico
Saving Sycamore by Molly B. Hudgens
The Secret Sauce by Rich Czyz
Shattering the Perfect Teacher Myth by Aaron Hogan
Stories from Webb by Todd Nesloney
Talk to Me by Kim Bearden
Teach Better by Chad Ostrowski, Tiffany Ott, Rae Hughart, and Jeff Gargas
Teach Me, Teacher by Jacob Chastain
Teach, Play, Learn! by Adam Peterson
The Teachers of Oz by Herbie Raad and Nathan Lang-Raad
TeamMakers by Laura Robb and Evan Robb

Through the Lens of Serendipity by Allyson Apsey
Write Here and Now by Dan Tricarico
The Zen Teacher by Dan Tricarico

Children's Books
The Adventures of Little Mickey by Mickey Smith Jr.
Alpert by LaNesha Tabb
Alpert & Friends by LaNesha Tabb
Beyond Us by Aaron Polansky
Cannonball In by Tara Martin
Dolphins in Trees by Aaron Polansky
Dragon Smart by Tisha and Tommy Richmond
I Can Achieve Anything by MoNique Waters
I Want to Be a Lot by Ashley Savage
The Magic of Wonder by Jenna Copper, Ashley Bible, Abby Gross, and Staci Lamb
Micah's Big Question by Naomi O'Brien
The Princes of Serendip by Allyson Apsey
Ride with Emilio by Richard Nares
A Teacher's Top Secret Confidential by LaNesha Tabb
A Teacher's Top Secret: Mission Accomplished by LaNesha Tabb
The Wild Card Kids by Hope and Wade King
Zom-Be a Design Thinker by Amanda Fox